"A fun read... packed with reasons for hope"

"Carl Kerby has challenged thousands to walk closer to Jesus and be a bold light in a dark world. His story will challenge you to look at your life and see how God takes the broken pieces of our lives and creates a masterpiece for the world to see."

MARK HALL, Casting Crowns

"It's so easy to see the passion behind your words when you speak about our Lord. And now that I've read *Reasons for Hope*, your life story reflects that passion. This is such an amazing story of hope, and urges readers to take belief in the Bible seriously and to be intentional about passing on that legacy to the next generation. Now more than ever, Christians need to know what they believe, why they believe it, and then be able to effectively communicate that in love. *Reasons for Hope* has encouraged me to do just that and is a book that I would recommend to every Christian."

MATT BUTLER, NewSong

"Carl's new book captures his heart for the lost and his sharp mind on critical issues facing our world. He knows what he's talking about and is able to teach others with humor, a quick wit, and solid scientific information. His story will inspire you and strengthen your faith."

KIRK CAMERON, actor and TV cohost

"It is difficult for me to differentiate between what I have gained from your book, and what I have gained from my personal relationship with you. You truly do practice what you preach! The two most important pieces of information I will take away from this book: stay bold and be prepared to give a defense of your faith. This book will inspire Christians to do just that. Your story, from your checkered childhood to your resistance to God's path for you, is a strong reminder that God has a plan for us all. Your explanation of how the Bible fits into the modern-day world, tackling issues such as evolution and race, is crucial to today's Christian."

RICH "ACE" FRANKLIN, three-time UFC MMA Champ

"From watching his dad's life as a pro wrestler to having people's lives in his hands as an air-traffic controller at one of the world's busiest airports, Carl Kerby has some stories to tell. *Reasons for Hope* is exactly what the title implies—an open and honest story of a young boy's journey from humble and challenging beginnings to a young man's new life in Christ, and then his calling by God into full-time ministry. Carl's journey and testimony provide encouragement and evidence of the power of God's love. A fun read...packed with reasons for hope."

TIM WILDMON, president, American Family Association (AFA) and American Family Radio

"As you read the 'mosaic' of Carl's life, you will appreciate the incredible understanding and knowledge he has about the youth in our culture today. Carl's passion will grow your passion and just maybe you will see how we can reach this Mosaic Generation with the truth of the gospel."

ERIC HOVIND, president, Creation Science Evangelism

REASONS
for HOPE

In the MOSAIC *of* Your Life

CARL KERBY

genesis
PUBLISHING GROUP

Reasons for Hope in the Mosaic of Your Life

Published by:
Genesis Publishing Group
2002 Skyline Place
Bartlesville, OK 74006
www.genesis-group.net

Edited by Shari Abbott and Lynn Copeland

Printed in the United States of America

ISBN 978-1-933591-09-4

Unless otherwise indicated, Scripture quotations are from the *New King James Version*, © 1979, 1980, 1982 by Thomas Nelson Inc., Publishers, Nashville, Tennessee.

Scripture quotations designated NASB are from *The New American Standard Bible*, © 1960, 1962, 1963, 1968, 1971, 1972, 1973, 1975, 1977, 1995 by The Lockman Foundation. Used by permission.

Scripture quotations designated NIV are from the *New International Version*, © 1973, 1978, 1984 by the International Bible Society. Published by Zondervan Bible Publishers, Grand Rapids, Michigan.

Scripture quotations designated Amplified are from *The Amplified Bible*, © 1965 by Zondervan Publishing House, Grand Rapids, Michigan.

Scripture quotations designated KJV are from the *King James Version*.

To those who don't have hope and need to be given it

to those who do have hope and need to share it

"Fear not, for I am with you; be not dismayed,
for I am your God. I will strengthen you, yes,
I will help you, I will uphold you with
My righteous right hand."
—ISAIAH 41:10

DEAR DIANNE & BILL,
THANK YOU FOR SUPPORTING
RFORTH. YOU ARE A BLESSING.
STAY BOLD,
[signature] ISA: 41:10-13
MERRY CHRISTMAS!

Contents

PART ONE
Offering Reasons for Hope in a Hopeless World

PART TWO
My Story: From Wrestler's Son to Professional Speaker

PART THREE
Answering Common Objections to the Christian Faith

Acknowledgments

What a journey! This book has taken over five years to come to fruition. And, honestly, the result isn't anything like I imagined. Praise God for that!

Above all, I thank my Lord and Savior Jesus Christ. He is my only true hope and He is the reason I am able to acknowledge the blessing of each of these people in my life. Without Him my life would be so very different.

First and foremost, I want to thank my wife, Masami. You truly are a gift from God. Your love for the Lord, and your love for me, are so humbling. There's no way this ministry exists without your support and encouragement. I praise God that He brought us together. I love you!

Marla Alupoaicei, thank you! You took a tangled mess of notes and ideas and made it better than I ever could have. God has given you an amazing gift!

Shari Abbott, I can never thank you enough. You do so much for Reasons for Hope (rforh)! Your work on this book has been amazing. From the insights that you've added (especially the Joshua stones section) to the vast amount of time you've spent editing this book, you have helped make it more powerful than I ever could have on my own. I appreciate your hard work, your gifts and wisdom that God has given you.

Candace Nordine, you are a blessing. Your loyalty and hard work blesses us so much. In addition to being a full-time wife and mother, what you do to make my life somewhat organized is amazing. Your family is inspiring and we love you guys.

My children and their spouses, Alisa and Bobby, Carl Jr. (Dennis) and Tish, I love you guys so much. Thank you for letting me share stories about you. Thank you for your patience and forgiveness for the numerous times that I failed you. Denny, a special thank you for all that you are doing for rforh. You are so gifted and it makes us so proud to see you use those talents for the Lord!

My grandbabyboy (yes, one word) Trey, you are a blessing. May the mistakes that I've made in life, from the testimonies of this book, help you learn early in life to love Jesus with all of your heart, soul, mind, and strength. We are praying that you will be an amazing warrior for the Lord Jesus Christ.

Dr. Robby Foster and Hopewell Baptist Church, thank you for sticking with me when rforh started in January 2011. I will never forget that!

Paul Gracey, Wade Wacker, and Dr. Randy Baker (the rforh board), you guys and your families so bless us with your support, wisdom, and friendship. I need it! I praise God for introducing us so that we are now serving the Lord Jesus Christ together.

Lynn Copeland, I don't know how you do all that you do. Your insights have had a huge impact on this book. Thank you for jumping in with us on this publication.

The Veracity Project—Bub Kuns, Charlie Matz, and Ian Royal Nelson—you guys are the best! I love you and am constantly amazed at the gifts God gave you.

Close friends James, Teri and Jimmy, Doug and Jackie and boys, Brian S. (love you, man!), Mark H. (thank you, sir!), Cherian & Mariamma J., Sylvan R., Dave L., Jeff G., Dave V., Bob and Dee, Kirk C., Tom M., Tim R., Jobe and Jenna Dee and girls, Britt and Shannon L., Jason P., my brother Stephan and Amber (you guys so bless me!), Rich and Beth F., Dr. Kroll, Mark C., and anyone I may have missed: without your support, rforh wouldn't exist. Thank you to all, even the ones I didn't have space to mention or forgot to add.

Foreword

Hanging on the wall of my family room is a beautiful mosaic Aztec calendar. It tells the story of time in pieces of wood of various sizes and colors. On the floor of the Byzantine church of St. George in Madaba, Jordan, is a mosaic map of the Holy Land. Dating from the sixth century A.D., it is the oldest surviving original cartograph depiction of the Holy Land and features an exquisite mosaic of Jerusalem. Several years ago I had an artisan in Jordan recreate that map of Jerusalem in a mosaic table that now has a prominent place in my study.

Images are important. Sometimes they help tell a story. Other times they are the story. Carl Kerby's life is a mosaic and in the pages that follow he uses the image of a mosaic to tell his story, or rather, God's story in his life.

God's story is the story of hope. Without God, there is no story of hope. When the apostle Paul wrote to the Christ-followers of Ephesus, he described what their life was like before they came to faith in Jesus Christ. Notice the mosaic of five phrases in this description: "At that time you were without Christ, being aliens from the commonwealth of Israel and strangers from the covenants of promise, having no hope and without God in the world" (Ephesians 2:12).

- without Christ
- aliens from the commonwealth of Israel
- strangers from the covenants of promise
- no hope
- without God

I do not know of two words that inject more terror into our lives than the words "no hope." Your oncologist calls you into her office for a private meeting. She announces that your cancer has spread throughout your body and there is "no hope." The police arouse you from sleep at 2:00 a.m. to tell you that your son was just involved in a serious automobile accident. He was rushed by ambulance to the hospital but there is "no hope."

Paul's description of the Gentiles in Ephesians 2:12 is the mosaic that was Carl Kerby's life. It was a mosaic of hopelessness. And then he discovered the hope that is found only in Jesus Christ. That's what the Ephesians discovered as well. Paul continued in verse 13, "But now in Christ Jesus you who once were far off have been brought near by the blood of Christ."

Carl's life is still a mosaic, but with different pieces. Mosaics are beautiful because each individual piece may have no beauty in itself, but place those inglorious pieces together and you have God's masterpiece.

As you read the chapters that follow, look for the mosaic. The chapters are pieces of the whole, the book is the whole. Let Carl's story encourage you in your own story, his mosaic give you hope for your own mosaic. God is still in the business of putting together life's pieces in ways that bring beauty to the plain, glory to the ordinary, and hope to the hopeless.

DR. WOODROW KROLL
Back to the Bible

Introduction

I have always been intrigued by mosaics—decorative designs created with small colored pieces of stone or tile. When I began to explore the history of mosaics, I was astonished to discover how long this art form has been around.

The ancient Sumerians first developed the technique of making mosaics around 3000 B.C. in Mesopotamia (now Iraq) using clay pegs. The Egyptians and the Greeks adapted the technique to make decorative objects, and later the Romans created even more elaborate mosaics by cutting pieces of colored stone into specific shapes to fit into larger designs.[1]

In a mosaic, the artist arranges small pieces of cut or broken stone or tile, called *tesserae*, to create a decorative pattern. We may struggle to grasp the overall design of a mosaic when we are looking at the individual pieces up close. All we see are what look like bits of junk, broken and useless. But when we step back far enough to view the entire mosaic, we gain a new perspective, and we can see the intricate beauty of the finished masterpiece. And that enables us to grasp the original intent of the artist.

Author Terry Tempest Williams says, "Shards of glass can cut and wound or magnify a vision. Mosaic celebrates brokenness and the beauty of being brought together."[2] God gave me this concept of mosaics, I believe, to help "magnify my vision" and illustrate why you and I must always be ready and equipped to give the reasons for our hope. I also use this concept of mosaics as a way to share my personal testimony during many of my messages and with people I meet.

Some time ago, the Lord helped me to see that my life is a mosaic, made from a bunch of broken, eclectic, and seemingly random pieces. As you delve into this book, you will discover how God brought me, the most unlikely of candidates, from darkness to light, and, ultimately, into a place where He could use me for His glory.

I will be interweaving several themes: my experiences growing up with a father who was a prominent professional wrestler; my journey from a rebellious young man to a follower of Christ; how God led me to become an air-traffic controller and then into a full-time speaking ministry; and, most important, how God established my firm belief that the Bible provides the answers we need as we wrestle with life's most difficult questions.

I am a redeemed sinner, saved by grace through faith in Jesus Christ. There's nothing special about me that uniquely qualifies me to encourage people and share the gospel with the lost. But that's exactly what the Lord has empowered me to do. He enabled me to be a part of a ministry where I am able to travel, speak, and share God's Word with people all over the world.

God, the artist of my life, has chosen to gather up those broken pieces and unique elements of my background, and He has put them together to make me a useful vessel for His work. And I know He will do the same for you!

PART ONE

Offering
REASONS FOR HOPE
in a Hopeless World

Rocks, Stones, Boulders, and Mosaics

C raig DeMartino had no clue that his life would change forever when he set out for Colorado's Rocky Mountains on July 21, 2002. A rock climber, Craig was doing what he loved best as he scaled the heights of the Sundance Buttress in Rocky Mountain National Park. Little did he know that the harrowing climb would be the last time he would plant both feet on a mountain.

After a tragic instant of miscommunication, Craig tumbled off the rocky cliff and plummeted nine stories to an almost certain death. Freefalling at over sixty miles per hour, he crashed onto the mountain floor—feet first. His boots exploded upon impact, and his feet and ankles were shattered. A powerful shockwave moved up his body, breaking his back and fracturing his neck. The fall also punctured a lung and tore a shoulder. After being evacuated to the hospital, Craig remained unconscious as the doctors advised his family that he had less than an hour to live.

But God had a different plan for Craig. Through a series of miraculous events, Craig survived his one-hundred-foot fall.

Although Craig didn't conquer the mountain by rock climbing, he did conquer the "rock" of difficulties that he faced after the accident, including the amputation of his right leg eighteen months later. Following his miraculous survival, and during his challenging recovery, he discovered a renewed relationship with Jesus Christ, which led to a passion for testifying of God's wondrous power in his life. He's even proven the overcoming power of God by the strength and perseverance he exhibited when he became the first amputee to climb the 3,000-foot face of El Capitan in Yosemite on June 5, 2006, just six weeks shy of the four-year anniversary of the accident.

No doubt, Craig's fall from the cliff was traumatic. But he recognized that his "rendezvous" with the rocks below was not an unforeseen accident in God's eyes, and that how he responded to his predicament would change the entire course of his life.

"I think that's how God works in our lives—there are no accidents, only things that work for the good of the kingdom," Craig writes. "I think that's the key to my attitude in general, that I know God uses everything that happens to me to further the kingdom. That on even the really bad days, and I have a lot of them, He is using the things I do, and you do, to make an impact somewhere. Even when I don't think that's happening, it is, and I usually see it down the road in ways I never could have imagined."[3]

I believe God knew Craig would suffer that fall, and He is the one who gave him the fortitude to survive the rocky ordeal. Because of that experience, Craig now encourages others to live their lives centered on Christ.[4]

All of us, like Craig, face challenges in our lives. How we deal with those challenges is what this book is all about. Do we use the stones, rocks and boulders of life to build a strong foundation or are we crushed by their weight?

Chapter 1

As I look back over the years, I can clearly see the stumbling stones and crushing rocks that were problems and obstacles in my life. But I can also see how God used them for His plan and purpose in my life—to build a foundation that has brought me to the place and person I am today. I grew up with an extremely unusual background as the son of a professional wrestler. Professional wrestling is a world that few know much about, and I'll be sharing the realities of that lifestyle, giving you a glimpse of that world, in the following chapters. My path has been a rocky one—struggling with a difficult childhood, dropping out of high school, even being homeless at one point. Some of the "boulders" in my life were disadvantages, but most of them were just difficult situations in which I made very poor choices. But you know what? None of those boulders surprised God. In fact, when I remember the negative experiences and failures from my past, I cling to this passage of Scripture:

> He also brought me up out of a horrible pit, out of the miry clay, and set my feet upon a rock, and established my steps. (Psalm 40:2)

And that "rock" is Jesus. This verse reminds me that I'm not the man that I used to be; God has created a new heart and new mind within me. He lifted me out of the mess that I was in and placed me on solid ground. My brothers and sisters in Christ, He's done the same for you!

THE BEAUTY OF MOSAICS

To me, a mosaic is such a fitting illustration of the way God can take the broken pieces of our lives and create something beautiful from them. My life has been filled with boulders and broken stones. Yet God, in His grace, has put those stones together in a mosaic to make me into a useful vessel for His use. I was privileged to serve for sixteen years with the ministry Answers in Genesis (AiG), teaching people that God's Word is true from the very first verse. In January 2011, with the help of some great friends, I founded a new ministry named Reasons for Hope, as a part of my desire to equip Christians to offer reasons for their spiritual hope to lost and dying people. That hope comes only from salvation through faith in Jesus Christ. I never would have imagined how my life would turn out, but God, the Grand Designer, has pieced together the good as well as the broken pieces of my life into an amazing mosaic.

The term "mosaic" also has another meaning. The "Mosaic Generation" describes the group of young people born between 1984 and 2002. Sometimes called Millennials, Generation Y, Echo Boom, or Generation Next, they are the newest of the five generations coexisting in society today. The others are the Baby Busters/Generation X (born 1965–1983); the Baby Boomers (1946–1964); the Builders (1927–1945); and the Seniors (1926 and prior; sometimes called Traditionalists or Matures).

Unfortunately, the meaning of "mosaic" used for this emerging generation is far different from mine. Instead of emphasizing how beauty can come from broken pieces, it seems they almost embrace the brokenness as normal.

Maybe more than any other generation today, those in the Mosaic Generation need to hear God's truth. Let me share with you some of the characteristics that are used to describe these Mosaics (so-called because of their multifaceted, eclectic lifestyles). First, they're "plugged in" to all types of technology and media. According to author David Kinnaman, Mosaics spend up to eight and a half hours every day using technology and media, often using two or three types simultaneously (such as listening to music while using the computer). In addition, Mosaics desire fresh, stimulating experiences and love to express their individuality. Twenty-five percent of Mosaics have posted personalized content online, including stories, videos, blogs, artwork, or photos of themselves. More importantly, those in the Mosaic Generation are nonlinear thinkers who are comfortable with contradiction and are morally pragmatic ("I'll do whatever works").[5]

For Mosaics, this philosophy of moral pragmatism typically is expressed in the following statements:

- What is right for you may not be right for me.

- I do what I think is best, not what anyone else thinks is best.

- You are the only one who can determine what is right and what is wrong.

- There is no absolute truth.[6]

Hopefully, if you have a biblical background, you can see immediately that these statements are at odds with Scripture. The Bible is clear that all of us have God's moral law (the Ten Commandments) written on our hearts to tell us what is right and what is wrong and to convict us of sin. The apostle Paul states in Romans 2:15 that men have "the work of the law written in their hearts, their conscience also bearing witness..." The Bible also tells us that God's Word is absolutely true and is our standard for living. The psalmist writes, "For the word of the LORD is right, and all His work is done in truth" (Psalm 33:4), and "Your word is a lamp to my feet and a light to my path" (Psalm 119:105). Surprisingly, only 6 percent of Mosaic teens who consider themselves to be "born again" have a biblical worldview (meaning that they believe in absolute truth, that the Bible is God's Word, that "Satan is real," "Jesus never sinned," and a handful of similar orthodox beliefs). That means the other 94 percent adhere in some way to a philosophy of moral pragmatism. Obviously, we have a lot of work to do as far as sharing the gospel with this generation.

However, the Mosaic Generation has many positive qualities, too. Mosaics have a joyful and positive outlook on life, and they long for personal connection and powerful experiences. They consider religion and spirituality to be a positive dimension of life, and they want to experience God's truth by building authentic relationships with other people who have faith in God. Most Mosaics agree with the statement that they are "looking for a few good friends." I would say that's true for most everyone in our culture today.

As we encounter those in the Mosaic Generation, we can follow Paul's approach in reaching the lost. He tells us in 1 Corinthians 9:22, "to the weak I became as weak, that I might win the weak. I have become all things to all men, that I might by all means save some." Paul never compromised his message or watered down the truth of the gospel, but boldly proclaimed, "For I am not ashamed of the gospel of Christ, for it is the power of God to salvation for everyone who believes…" (Romans 1:16). He was always faithful in proclaiming saving grace, so when Paul spoke of becoming "all things to all men," he was talking about trying to relate to the lost in the best way he could in order to reach them with the gospel. He tried to understand who they were, and be kind and courteous in his approach to witness to them. For example, to those who are "weak" in the knowledge of the Lord and the gospel, Paul "became as weak," meaning he met them at their level of knowledge and added to their understanding by proclaiming Christ to them. To those who don't believe in absolute truth, we can start by addressing their current beliefs and then help them see their need for the One who is Truth.

That's what I want to help you do in this book: to help you become "all things to all men." No matter which generations you and I may be in, we need to speak the truth of the gospel in love, be patient and understanding, and show people the need for Jesus Christ and His Word. The gospel must always be the primary focus of our message, but we can support our proclamation of the gospel with our personal testimony as well. We can share with people how God has worked in our lives. By sharing our testimonies we can often connect to others in a deeper way and help them to come to an understanding of the reasons for hope found only in Jesus Christ.

READY TO SHARE

On my travels I often have the opportunity to meet fascinating people who need the gospel. One of the most memorable was a professor I met while speaking in Kentucky. He teaches global warming at a university in England, and his sister (who is a Christian) had invited him to come with her to hear me speak.

After my talk, he and I had a dynamic discussion about the topics I had addressed, including the theory of global warming. He disagreed with me on quite a few points, but I was open to his ideas and questions. We had a good time dialoguing back and forth and challenging each other to provide evidence for our positions.

One influential person I had mentioned in my talk that day was Richard Dawkins, an anti-Christian activist and one of the strongest proponents of the theory of evolution and the "New Atheism" movement. I have never met Dawkins personally, but from what I have seen in interviews, he is an angry man. He hates Christians, and he seems to "have it out" for the Christian community and anyone who believes in God, creation, or intelligent design. To give you an example, consider the titles of some of the books Dawkins has penned:

- *The God Delusion*

- *The Blind Watchmaker: Why the Evidence of Evolution Reveals a Universe without Design*

- *The Greatest Show on Earth: The Evidence for Evolution*
- *Everything You Know About God is Wrong: The Disinformation Guide to Religion* (contributor)

As I prepared to leave, this British professor told me, "You know, you're not what I expected!"

I laughed and said, "I could take that a couple of ways. What do you mean?"

He told me, "I expected you to be angry and want to argue with me because I don't agree with you."

"I don't hate you because you don't think like I do," I replied. "In fact, I spent many years believing the same things that you do. But God doesn't tell us to fight or argue. He just tells us to be ready to share with others the reason for our hope. So that's what I do!"

I continued, "When I see people harboring so much anger and hatred toward others who are supposedly so 'stupid' and 'uninformed,' I just don't understand it. Think about Richard Dawkins. Why is he so angry? If he truly believes Christians are so stupid, he should feel sorry for us. For example, if someone walked up to me and told me that he believed the moon was made of green cheese, and he was totally sincere, would I get angry and fight with him or call him names? No way. I'd pat him on the back and say, 'I love you, brother, but you may want to go get some help!' The fact that Richard Dawkins is so angry shows me that the Holy Spirit is working on him. I'm praying for him. I still believe there is hope for him!"

I told the professor that I had really enjoyed meeting him and discussing science and Scripture with him. We shook hands and parted ways. I prayed that he would consider the truths I had shared with him.

About three months later, I received an email from this same professor. He said, "Carl, you won't believe this, but I trusted Jesus Christ as my Savior the Sunday after I met you!"

Wow! I thought. This news caught me totally off guard, but I was thrilled to hear it.

His email continued: "You know what else? What really got me was what you shared about Richard Dawkins. You didn't know this, but not long before I heard you speak, I had actually posted this on my Facebook page: 'Richard Dawkins is God.'"

I was blown away by this man's testimony. Only the living God can take someone from believing "Richard Dawkins is God" to proclaiming "Jesus Christ is Lord"! This man's Christian sister had been witnessing to him and praying for him for years. I'm sure God heard her prayers and prepared his heart to be receptive to the gospel that day.

I'm humbled and awed that God allows you and me to play a small role in helping people like this man realize that God's Word is true and that it is our standard for living. The apostle Paul wrote that we are to cast "down arguments and every high thing that exalts itself against the knowledge of God," and that we are to bring every thought captive to the obedience of Christ (2 Corinthians 10:5). God has the power and the will to tear down any argument or speculation that opposes the truth of His Word. I believe that's what happened that day. The stumbling stones that had been in place for years in this man's life were removed when he simply heard the truth spoken in love.

JOSHUA AND THE MEMORIAL STONES

The concept of mosaics really begins to take shape as we consider the purpose of memorial stones in Scripture. The Bible contains powerful examples of stone memorials that people built to help them remember how God had worked in their lives.

Let's start by focusing on the life of Joshua. This biblical leader was my type of guy; he knew how to get things done! Remember, as the Israelites anticipated entering the Promised

Land, Moses sent twelve men to spy on the land of Canaan and report back with their findings (Numbers 13). Joshua was one of those twelve men. Despite the fact that the cities were well fortified and it seemed impossible for the Israelites to overcome the Canaanites, Joshua and Caleb were ready to go for it. In Numbers 14 we read Joshua and Caleb's response: "If the LORD delights in us, then He will bring us into this land and give it to us, 'a land which flows with milk and honey.' Only do not rebel against the LORD, nor fear the people of the land, for they are our bread; their protection has departed from them, and the LORD is with us. Do not fear them." Of the twelve men, Joshua and Caleb were the only two who maintained a faith that God would lead them into the land He had promised. Based on the report of the other ten, Israel did not enter the Promised Land and instead was consigned to wander forty years in the wilderness until the nonbelieving generation had passed away.

After the forty years of wandering, Joshua assumed the leadership of the Israelites following Moses' death, and led them into the land. Joshua faced fierce battles, leadership struggles, and (of course) plenty of grumbling and complaining from the Israelite people. But he had earned the great privilege of leading God's people into the Promised Land and he remained faithful to God through it all.

One of my favorite Bible passages contains the Lord's powerful words to Joshua:

> "Have I not commanded you? Be strong and of good courage; do not be afraid, nor be dismayed, for the LORD your God is with you wherever you go." (Joshua 1:9)

During the time of Joshua's leadership, the Lord commanded His people to use stones to serve as memorials. These memorials commemorated times when God performed miracles and showered grace upon His people even though they didn't deserve it (which, after all, is the definition of grace!). In Joshua 4, God told the Israelites that these memorials would serve as a sign to them and that when their children would ask, "What do these stones mean to you?" they would recount how God had miraculously provided. In a way, these assembled stones were similar to mosaics, creating a picture to remind each generation of God's faithfulness and provision.

The Israelites enjoyed gathering together to celebrate special feasts and festivals, just like we do at Easter, Thanksgiving, and Christmas. But they didn't celebrate just because it was fun. God commanded them to build memorials so that they would never forget His mercy and grace and to celebrate His goodness and faithfulness to them. He wanted the Israelites to remember all the ways that He had worked in their lives in the past.

I believe the same is true today. We should use the "stones" of hardships in our lives as reminders of what God has done for us, sharing them with the current generation so that they will be able to share with future generations the "stones" from their lives.

Chapter 3 of the book of Joshua records how God miraculously enabled His people to cross the Jordan River on dry land. He wanted to build up the Israelites' faith and courage to show them that He would give them victory in battle over their enemies. Joshua said to the Israelites:

> "Come here, and hear the words of the LORD your God. By this you shall know that the living God is among you, and that He will without fail drive out from before you the Canaanites and the Hittites and the Hivites and the Perizzites and the Girgashites and the Amorites and the Jebusites: Behold, the ark of the covenant of the Lord of all the earth is crossing over before you into the Jordan. Now therefore, take for yourselves twelve men from the

tribes of Israel, one man from every tribe. And it shall come to pass, as soon as the soles of the feet of the priests who bear the ark of the LORD, the Lord of all the earth, shall rest in the waters of the Jordan, that the waters of the Jordan shall be cut off, the waters that come down from upstream, and they shall stand as a heap." (Joshua 3:9–13)

In the following verses, we discover something surprising about the Jordan River: it is at flood stage all through the harvest. Yet here's what happened:

> …as those who bore the ark came to the Jordan, and the feet of the priests who bore the ark dipped in the edge of the water (for the Jordan overflows all its banks during the whole time of harvest), that the waters which came down from upstream stood still, and rose in a heap very far away at Adam, the city that is beside Zaretan. So the waters that went down into the Sea of the Arabah, the Salt Sea, failed, and were cut off; and the people crossed over opposite Jericho. Then the priests who bore the ark of the covenant of the LORD stood firm on dry ground in the midst of the Jordan; and all Israel crossed over on dry ground, until all the people had crossed completely over the Jordan. (Joshua 3:15–17)

Does this ring a bell? It reminds me of the time when God worked a miracle and enabled Moses to lead over two million Israelites across the Red Sea on dry ground as they escaped from slavery in Egypt. Now, God was showing His people that He was still in control by performing a similar miracle under the leadership of Joshua. (By the way, aren't we glad that He's still in control today?)

I love what happens next; now we're getting to the "memorial stones" section. As a reminder to the current and future generations of what a great thing God had done for His people, God commanded Joshua to build a memorial. Twelve men (one from each tribe) went to the riverbed, and each removed one stone. They carried these stones to where they camped on the western side of the Jordan and piled them up as a memorial.

In addition, God commanded Joshua to build a second memorial—a pile of stones right in the middle of the Jordan River! Joshua picked up stones and carried them to the place where the ark of the covenant was still stationed and "set up twelve stones" in the midst of the riverbed (Joshua 4:9). (Why would God tell Joshua to set stones in the middle of the river, since they would quickly be covered when the water started to flow again? See the sidebar for the amazing answer.)

> *The stones "cry out" the message to every generation that God is steadfast in His promises to deliver and bless His people.*

The Jordan crossing was an amazing miracle of God, a sign to His people that He was the One who led them into the land. This miracle was to give them faith that He would also lead them into battle against the Canaanites and that He would empower them to possess the land (Joshua 3:9–13). The stone memorial on the riverbank testified to His faithfulness and served as a reminder to them and future generations that only God is their deliverer and their source of strength. The stones "cry out" the message to every generation that God is steadfast in His promises to deliver and bless His people.

Joshua's "Underwater Memorial"

Remember that throughout the Old Testament, God provided signs to his people to reveal Himself, His plans, and especially the promise of a coming Messiah. The book of Joshua begins with the people preparing to enter the Promised Land, their God-given inheritance. They are not led by Moses, who represents the Law, but by Joshua, an Old Testament picture and foreshadow of our Savior, who is the only way to our inheritance.

We read in Joshua 3:17 that the ark stood firm on dry ground in the middle of the Jordan while the people passed through untouched by the waters of the Jordan. Often in the Bible we see where water serves as a symbol of the wrath or judgment of God: the Flood (Genesis 6:17; Hebrews 11:7); the Red Sea drowning of the Egyptians (Exodus 14:28; Hebrews 11:29); Jonah going under the waters (Jonah 1; 2:3). Even the word "Jordan" implies judgment. A. W. Pink breaks the word into two Hebrew roots: *jor* or *yar*, which is literally "spread," and *dan*, which means "judging" (Genesis 30:6). Others define it as *yar-dane*, meaning "descender." Baptism, where the person is immersed in water and risen to new life by the power of Christ, is also a picture of the old man being judged by God, dying to self, and being saved by Christ. Jesus' followers are commissioned to be "fishers of men" (Matthew 4:19; Mark 1:17), and the Psalms confirm our being taken out from the waters:

> He sent from above, He took me; He drew me out of many waters. (Psalm 18:16)

Deliver me out of the mire, and let me not sink; let me be delivered from those who hate me, and out of the deep waters. Let not the floodwater overflow me, nor let the deep swallow me up; and let not the pit shut its mouth on me. (Psalm 69:14,15)

"If it had not been the LORD who was on our side," let Israel now say—"If it had not been the LORD who was on our side, when men rose up against us, then they would have swallowed us alive, when their wrath was kindled against us; then the waters would have overwhelmed us, the stream would have gone over our soul; then the swollen waters would have gone over our soul." (Psalm 124:1–5)

"I will pour out My wrath on them like water." (Hosea 5:10)

In Joshua 4, God instructed the twelve men (one from each tribe) to take a stone from the middle of the dry riverbed to build a memorial on the west bank of the Jordan. These stones came from the place that pictures death, the miry bottom of a riverbed. They had been buried beneath the waters, the picture of wrath and judgment. The "ark of the LORD," which is a picture of Christ (in both construction and in being the place where God dwelled among His people) stood in the midst of the Jordan, allowing these stones to be brought up out of the waters (death) to create a memorial of deliverance (redemption). Remember, this was done "that this may be a sign among you..." (Joshua 4:6).

We read in Joshua 4:9 that it was Joshua, not the twelve, who was told to "set up twelve stones in the midst of the

Jordan, in the place where the feet of the priests who bore the ark of the covenant stood; and they are there to this day." This is a picture of the unredeemed, those who die in their sin, who are buried in death by the righteous judgment of God—"and they are there to this day" (Joshua 4:9). What a frightening thought and a reminder to all of us to be bold in sharing the saving grace of the gospel.

The twelve stones taken out from the Jordan depths and placed on dry ground "where they lodged" (Joshua 4:8) symbolize those who were redeemed by Christ (the ark) and came out from under the judgment of God (the waters) to new life in the Promised Land (inheritance of life in Christ). And remember that the people crossed over the Jordan at the time of Passover! This was at the "time of harvest" (Joshua 3:15), "on the tenth day of the first month" (Joshua 4:19). This is a beautiful picture of the saving grace of Jesus Christ.

The Joshua 4 memorial also reminds us of a future promise given in Isaiah 43:2, where God says, "When you pass through the waters, I will be with you; and through the rivers, they shall not overflow you." Notice that promise says "when," not "if." We all know that in this life trials will come our way, and we must always remember that He promises to be with us, to deliver us, to set our feet on solid ground. Remember the verse:

> He also brought me up out of a horrible pit, out of the miry clay, and set my feet upon a rock, and established my steps. (Psalm 40:2)

2

Why Everyone Needs Hope

J ust as memorial stones cause us to consider how God can build our lives to bring honor and glory to Him, mosaics give us a tangible way to understand how God can transform us from something broken into something beautiful and valuable. God can use our story of brokenness to give people encouragement and hope in their own lives. In order to bring hope to others, I want to be faithful in sharing all that God has done for me.

One day, as I was reading Mark chapter 5 about the demon-possessed man in Gadara, I began to identify with his testimony. Here's the scene:

> And when He [Jesus] had come out of the boat, immediately there met Him out of the tombs a man with an unclean spirit, who had his dwelling among the tombs; and no one could bind him, not even with chains, because he had often been bound with shackles and chains. And the chains had been pulled apart by him, and the shackles broken in pieces; neither could anyone tame him.

And always, night and day, he was in the mountains and in the tombs, crying out and cutting himself with stones.

When he saw Jesus from afar, he ran and worshiped Him. And he cried out with a loud voice and said, "What have I to do with You, Jesus, Son of the Most High God? I implore You by God that You do not torment me."

For He said to him, "Come out of the man, unclean spirit!" Then He asked him, "What is your name?"

And he answered, saying, "My name is Legion; for we are many." Also he begged Him earnestly that He would not send them out of the country.

Now a large herd of swine was feeding there near the mountains. So all the demons begged Him, saying, "Send us to the swine, that we may enter them." And at once Jesus gave them permission. Then the unclean spirits went out and entered the swine (there were about two thousand); and the herd ran violently down the steep place into the sea, and drowned in the sea.

So those who fed the swine fled, and they told it in the city and in the country. And they went out to see what it was that had happened. Then they came to Jesus, and saw the one who had been demon-possessed and had the legion, sitting and clothed and in his right mind. And they were afraid. And those who saw it told them how it happened to him who had been demon-possessed, and about the swine. Then they began to plead with Him to depart from their region.

And when He got into the boat, he who had been demon-possessed begged Him that he might be with Him. (Mark 5:2–18)

I find it fascinating that the people who didn't "get it" wanted Jesus to leave, but the man who was healed begged to stay with Jesus. He wanted to follow the Lord, but that wasn't God's plan. Our heavenly Father had an even better design for this man's life—one that would allow the good news to reach many more people. Jesus said to the man:

> "Go home to your friends, and tell them what great things the Lord has done for you, and how He has had compassion on you." And he departed and began to proclaim in Decapolis all that Jesus had done for him; and all marveled. (Mark 5:19,20)

Through this book, I want to take the opportunity to do the same thing—to tell you how Jesus has healed me and transformed my life. If you know Christ as your Savior, my prayer is that this book will encourage you to share how God has radically changed your life as well. I'll be sharing some "memorial stones" from the mosaic of my own life and the lives of others. I pray you'll be inspired by how Jesus Christ has transformed each of us.

If you do not already know Jesus as your Savior, then my greatest desire as I share these truths with you is that you will realize that there truly is a God and He works in amazing ways. He can take all the broken shards of your life and make you into a new creation—a beautiful mosaic. And once you have established a relationship with Christ, then I want to challenge you to be a memorial to His goodness and faithfulness by being bold and confident in telling other people what the Lord has done in your life.

THERE'S NO PLACE LIKE HOME

Over the past few years, I've had the privilege of traveling more than one hundred and eighty days a year doing ministry. I've spoken to groups as small as six and as large as nine thousand. But I've noticed that regardless of the size of the audience, people everywhere have the same desires and issues in common.

One fact I've observed in my travels is this: we live in a culture that is becoming increasingly dark and hopeless. People desperately need God's hope and redemption, but in these politically correct times, Christians are more hesitant than ever to share their faith.

This doesn't make sense to me. Over the past year, my ministry travels have taken me to the Philippines, Japan, and England on multiple occasions. And what I've discovered, to borrow a phrase from Dorothy in *The Wizard of Oz*, is that "There's no place like home!" America is a blessed nation, to say the least. So why is there so much hopelessness and despair? And for those of us who know the joy of Christ, why would we not want to share our joy and blessings with others?

Take a typical Thanksgiving or Christmas here at home. We'll eat more food in a single meal than half of the world has access to in a week or a month, or, in some cases, even a year! Most of us live in beautiful homes with all the comforts a person could imagine. We have clean water to drink and food in the fridge. We have air-conditioning in the summer and heat in the winter. We have closets full of clothes. I'm embarrassed to admit this, but I've got clothes in my closet that I haven't worn in over a year. (That's because I don't like them. I probably can't even fit into them anymore, but that's beside the point.) I've got so many shirts I can *choose* which one to wear, while millions of people around the globe have nothing to wear at all.

Most important, we have the freedom to go to whatever place of worship we choose, on whichever day of the week we desire, without the fear of persecution or repercussions.

Why then do we see such a dark cloud of hopelessness covering our great nation today? Why and how could there be so much darkness in a country that has been blessed exceedingly abundantly? What is happening that is causing a great nation like ours to suffer and stumble? In the face of this darkness, why are Christians too embarrassed or afraid to share their faith? It just doesn't make sense.

According to the 2010 census, the U.S. population is approximately 310 million.[7] It's also estimated that we have close to 400,000 churches nationwide. Some cities have a church on nearly every corner. Because of all these churches, many people claim that we are the most "Christian" nation in the world today. But are we really? It's true that we have more Christian TV, more Christian radio stations, more Christian books, and more Christian music than any time in history. We even have Christian T-shirts, shoes, wristbands, bookmarks, earrings, and more! You name it, we've got it, and it's all "Christian." We even have "Christian" neckties! A friend of mine calls these products "Jesus junk" (in a loving way, of course).

Speaking of ties, would you like to hear my theology on that? Let me be honest; I have to admit up front that I'm biased. I'd much prefer to wear a Hawaiian shirt and shorts than a suit and tie. Now, I know I'm walking on thin ice here, and some of you are probably going to put this book down after you hear my opinion about neckties. But here goes!

Let me tell you why I don't like ties, and it's totally biblical. In my humble opinion, when you wear a tie, you are celebrating the curse of Adam! Think about it; there were no ties prior to Adam sinning, were there? You can't argue with me on that point. Nobody was wearing ties in the Garden.

Next, I can tell you where ties came from. In Genesis 4:15, we read that after Cain killed his brother Abel, God put a "mark" on Cain. Now, the Bible never says what that mark was. (Forget about skin color; that has nothing to do with it. By the way, we'll deal with that subject later in this book.) If you ask me, God "marked" Cain by putting a tie around his neck! That may sound silly, but you can't prove me wrong until we get to heaven, so I'm sticking to my little bit of "tie-ology."

Of course, I'm joking about ties. But there's one thing that I'm not joking about. If we truly have approximately 400,000 churches in America, and most of those churches are filled with "believers," then why don't we see more of their influence on the culture around us?

If the church were filled with folks who truly believed what they said they believed and who lived out their faith reflecting those beliefs, it would be having a tremendous impact across our nation. Yet in the midst of our prosperity, we see waves of hopelessness crashing all around us, as illustrated by the increasing rates of divorce, sexual perversion, depression, suicide, etc. Something is definitely not right in America.

In the midst of our prosperity, we see waves of hopelessness crashing all around us. Something is definitely not right in America.

Let me further illustrate it like this. There are approximately 6,000 first-run movie theaters across America. Now, let's be honest: which institution impacts the culture more? Is it the 400,000 churches, or is it the 6,000 movie theaters? No contest—it's the theaters. And those theaters primarily show movies that promote a secular worldview based on humanistic beliefs. Humanism teaches that we are on this earth to get all the possessions and enjoy all the pleasures we can; that we are nothing but an accident, a product of evolution's random processes; that what is wrong with this world can be righted with more education and government; that man is supreme rather than our omnipotent sovereign Lord and Savior Jesus Christ.

Chapter 2

THE PROPER BASIS FOR OUR HOPE

In our society's struggle between biblical Christianity and secular humanism, Christians need to be more ready than ever to offer hope to a world without it. The apostle Peter writes that we are to always have a ready answer to defend our faith:

> But sanctify the Lord God in your hearts: and be ready always to give an answer to every man that asketh you a reason of the hope that is in you ... (1 Peter 3:15, KJV)

I want to emphasize the fact that in this verse God is not *suggesting* that we be prepared to give answers. He is *commanding* us to be prepared to give answers.

The first step in preparation, Peter says, is to "sanctify the Lord God in your hearts." The word "sanctify" comes from the Greek word *hagiazo*, which means to make holy, purify, or consecrate. Other translations say to "give honor" or "revere." The word "revere" means "to show devoted deferential honor to; regard as worthy of great honor" and comes from the Latin *revereri*, meaning "to fear, respect."[8] This is serious business. The apostle Peter, as he is led by the Holy Spirit to write this verse, shows that it is vitally important to be prepared to share our faith as well as to "sanctify," or give honor to, the Lord. If Peter takes it this seriously, we should as well.

Peter was writing to people who were suffering some of the most severe persecution this world has ever known because of their faith. But even in the midst of this persecution, God didn't tell them to hide away in a "Christian bubble" from the big, bad world. God wanted His followers to be visible, bright shining lights in the midst of a dark culture. And I believe He wants us to do the same today. This message should still be proclaimed in our churches.

God's people are called to be a "holy people" (Deuteronomy 14:2). Some verses even call God's own a "peculiar people," meaning not that we are weird, but that we are set apart to shine His light and to do His work. When people see us, hear us, and watch how we act, they should immediately be able to tell that there is something different about us. Trust me when I say that you cannot be any more "peculiar" than when you stand on the truth of the Word of God and proclaim the name of Jesus in the midst of all the sin and compromise that we see in our culture today.

A key to standing firm in the midst of compromise is realizing that the Bible isn't a book of fairy tales or fables simply dealing with spiritual and moral issues. It is actually one of the most accurate history books ever written, from the only One who's always been there and who knows everything that has ever happened in this world. We can trust the Bible from the very beginning all the way to the end because, ultimately, it is the perfect and complete Word of God.

First Thessalonians 2:13 says, "For this reason we also thank God without ceasing, because when you received the word of God which you heard from us, you welcomed it not as the word of men, but as it is in truth, the word of God, which also effectively works in you who believe."

I am still amazed that God has chosen us—fallen, fallible, broken, but redeemed, sinners—to serve Him by sharing His unconditional love and grace with a lost and dying world. When we do not share the reason for our hope, not only are we being disobedient, we're missing out on one of the most incredible blessings of being a Christian. I've found that there is no greater joy than seeing a person receive real hope for the first time by trusting in Jesus Christ for salvation.

Genesis 1:1 says, "In the beginning God created the heaven and the earth" (KJV). When we know that we can fully trust Genesis 1:1, then we know that we can fully trust John 3:16: "For God so loved the world that He gave His only begotten

Son, that whoever believes in Him should not perish but have everlasting life." That means we can also trust in some of the most profound words that were ever spoken, when Jesus cried out from the cross as He was dying for our sins: "Father, forgive them, for they do not know what they do" (Luke 23:34).

God's love is so awe-inspiring that you and I will never be able to fully understand it this side of heaven. God loved me even when I was a sinner. He sent His Son, Jesus, to earth to willingly die on a cross for me. While I was spitting on Him and driving the nails into His wrists and feet, He loved me and died for me. And guess what? He did the same for you!

My friends, we don't need any more pewsitters. We need bold individuals living out what they believe. Why? Because *everyone needs hope.* The hope that comes only from knowing Jesus. We can't live without it! God has hardwired humans with the capacity for hope and the desire to cling to it even in the most painful and seemingly hopeless situations.

But there is a big difference between temporal (earthly) hope and eternal (heavenly) hope. Many of us have tried to find temporal hope by placing our trust in people, relationships, status, or material things. You may have spent your life desperately trying to gain acceptance or unconditional love from others, but you've been hurt and disappointed over and over. Such heartbreaks might cause you to withdraw and turn inward, or they might send you deeper into a downward spiral of despair and insecurity. *Will I ever find someone to love me?* you may be asking yourself. God did not create us to live our lives in isolation or depression, but rather to find our identity and worth in who we are in Him.

Others of us may have placed our hope in wealth, status, and power. You may have tried to climb the corporate ladder only to be passed over for a promotion, laid off, or replaced by a younger version of yourself. Or maybe you've tried to buy hope and satisfaction by shopping, but you always feel disappointed when you discover that material things bring conditional contentment only, and the feeling of euphoria that they give is short-lived. Too often we focus on things that are fleeting or temporal and miss those things that will last for eternity. God clearly warns us not to "love the world" because it is "passing away." However, the "one who does the will of God abides forever" (1 John 2:15–17).

The truth is, only those of us who know Jesus Christ as our Lord and Savior know what it's like to have an eternal, all-sufficient hope that will never disappoint. The Bible says that when we place our trust in Jesus for salvation, we have laid a solid spiritual foundation on the chief Cornerstone (Ephesians 2:20), the everlasting Rock who will never be shaken. Paul confirms in 1 Corinthians 10:4 that Jesus is our Rock: "For they drank of that spiritual Rock that followed them, and that Rock was Christ."

In his wonderful psalm of praise, King David declares, "The LORD is my rock and my fortress, and my deliverer; my God, my strength, in whom I will trust..." (Psalm 18:2).

And Psalm 130:7 says to "hope in the LORD; for with the LORD there is mercy, and with Him is abundant redemption."

The only way that anyone can gain abundant redemption, and eternal life, is to have Jesus as the rock-solid basis of our hope.

Sharing the Reasons for Your Hope: The Basics of Apologetics

You are probably familiar with the term "apologetics." This word sounds similar to the English word "apology," so some people may think that apologetics means we are "apologizing" for our faith. To be honest, I've heard many Christians share their faith in a timid way that sounded like they were apologizing. But let me ask you this: if you were swimming in the ocean with your best friend and he began to drown, and you grabbed him and helped him swim safely to shore, would you apologize afterward? Would you say, "Hey, buddy, sorry for saving your life"? No! Most likely, he would thank you repeatedly for what you had done for him.

Now, if you know Jesus Christ as your Lord and Savior, and you know that only Jesus can save your friend's life *forever* by giving him forgiveness of sin, a personal relationship with God, and the blessing of going to heaven when he dies, would you *apologize* for telling your friend the good news? Of course not. You'd be excited to tell him the truth. In the same way, we should be shouting God's truth from the rooftops instead of refusing to share it with people.

So although the words "apologetics" and "apology" sound similar, they don't both mean "to say you're sorry." Apologetics is something I'm excited about because I love people, and I want to see every person in the world come to a saving knowledge of Jesus Christ. The Lord has blessed my life and given me His hope that "does not disappoint" (Romans 5:5) despite the sins, failures, wrong turns, and disadvantages I faced early in my life. Trust me; because God saved me and turned my life around, I know that He desires to save everyone! We also have assurance of that from His Word (1 Timothy 2:4; 2 Peter 3:9).

If we can't explain why we believe what we do, and if we can't describe how God has changed our lives, then how can we possibly expect other people to want to embrace faith in Christ?

As I mentioned earlier, being able to give an answer for our faith is not a suggestion; it's a requirement! Those of us who are true Christ followers have the responsibility of being able to give reasonable explanations for the hope that we have. We should be able to state clearly what we believe and why we believe it. If we can't explain why we believe what we do, and if we can't describe how God has changed our lives, then how can we possibly expect other people to want to embrace faith in Christ?

And, even more importantly, if we can't articulate the saving grace that we received when Christ saved us, will there come a day when we question our own salvation? We are currently losing the majority of the young people raised in the church today. Do you think that maybe, just maybe, we're not "losing" them, but maybe we never "had" them? And maybe we never had them because they never truly knew what they believed to begin with?

If you could talk with the number of Christians around the world that I have, you would quickly find that very few can give a reason for the hope that is in them. I can't emphasize enough how important it is to be able to give an answer, to have knowledge and understanding.

Think about this for a moment. In Jesus' day, four- to five-year-old children started attending elementary school (Beth Sefer) in the local synagogue and they would memorize large portions of the Torah.

At approximately age thirteen when it became time to move on to secondary school (Beth Midrash), only the best students would continue with their studies. These students would continue their study of the Torah but would also begin to study the prophets and the writings alongside the adults. They also began to study the oral Torah so that they would know how to correctly interpret the Torah and began to study a trade. (The students who didn't make it to Beth Midrash would find a trade to begin their work life.)

At this point the students who excelled in their studies would be encouraged to seek a rabbi, with whom they would travel. If they passed the rabbi's test they would begin to travel with him, and learn directly from him. These students were called *talmidim* and they were more than just good students.

Good students want to learn from the teacher; the *talmidim* didn't just want to learn from the teacher, they wanted to become just like the teacher. It's been said that the *talmidim* wanted to look like, talk like, walk like, even smell like their rabbi! If the rabbi walked with a limp, you could tell his *talmidim* because they walked with a limp! Now, we don't know what Jesus "smelled" like, but we know how He spoke and what He taught because we have a record of it in the Word of

God. And the twelve that Jesus chose truly desired to be just like their Rabbi.

Remember also that Jesus turned the world upside down with twelve plain, ordinary men. They were men who at the age of twelve were passed over for the Beth Midrash. And remember, they didn't seek Jesus out, He sought them! These men were Jesus' *talmidim* and by their simple obedience they are a picture to us today of what it means to be truly committed to Jesus.

Jesus is seeking truly committed followers who, just like the *talmidim*, desire to follow in His footsteps, to walk in His ways. He is calling us to be *talmidim*, world changers. You cannot "turn the world upside down" if you can't give basic answers for your faith. Please hear me, this was important to Jesus' *talmidim* and it's important to me. When you come to a saving faith in Jesus Christ, you take His name. You become an ambassador on this earth for Him. Do not take His name in vain, in a meaningless way. Be committed to Him, your Rabbi, and prepare yourself to be ready and able to give an answer, a reason for the hope within you—then you'll truly be a "world changer" for Him!

Because there's nothing more important in life than helping others find the Savior, let's get started in understanding the basics of apologetics, so that we can share the reasons for our hope with a lost and dying world.

WHAT IS APOLOGETICS?

The English word "apologetics" comes from the Greek word *apologia*, which means "a well-reasoned reply; a *thought-out response* to adequately address the issue(s) that is raised; a *reasoned argument* (*defense*) that presented *evidence* (supplied *compelling proof*)."[9] *Apologia* is "the term for making a legal defense in an ancient court."[10] You can think of apologetics today as giving the evidence of our faith, defending it in the court of pubic opinion. My simple definition of apologetics is this: being ready and able to tell other people how Jesus has radically transformed my life and what the Bible says about God's offer of salvation.

Let's also consider what apologetics is *not*. With a bit of humor, Ryan Turner writes that apologetics is not:

■ The art of getting really good at saying, "I'm sorry!" over and over.

■ The art of intellectually forcing unbelievers into submission holds MMA [Mixed Martial Arts] style.

■ Arguing about how many angels can stand on a pin.[11]

The purpose of apologetics is not to judge people or argue with them, but to explain God's truth in a loving way that they can understand. We need to be able to share the gospel in a compelling manner that will cause people to want to know more about the Savior. God created people to walk in fellowship with Him. When we share the truth with them, we are simply helping them discover how they can have a loving, saving relationship with their Creator—the relationship that, deep down, everyone longs for, and the relationship that everyone was meant to have.

UNDERSTANDING THE BASICS

Some people consider Peter to be the apostle of hope. Perhaps this is because he grew to be a mighty man of faith despite the fact that he was a simple fisherman with no formal education. He denied Jesus three times, yet he became one of the most influential and courageous apostles. Peter's story gives me hope because it reveals that our God is a God of mercy, grace, forgiveness, and—best of all—second chances.

In his first epistle, Peter challenges his readers to make a bolder stand for the Lord Jesus Christ. Let's look again at 1 Peter 3:15 to learn how we can do that:

> But sanctify the Lord God in your hearts: and be ready always to give an answer to every man that asketh you a reason of the hope that is in you... (KJV)

To fully understand this verse and be able to apply it, we first need to know the context in which it was written. We've got to understand *to whom* it was being written and *why*.

First, *to whom* was Peter writing? As mentioned in the previous chapter, he was writing to believers who were suffering persecution. We think we suffer "persecution" today because television programs make fun of Christians or somebody calls us a nasty name. But these brothers and sisters in Christ were being imprisoned, persecuted, ostracized, tortured, and even killed for their faith. Their families were suffering.

Seeking to escape persecution, the believers of that time had spread throughout what is now modern-day Turkey. Peter was writing to encourage them to live holy lives in the midst of this persecution. He was calling his fellow believers to live lives that would glorify God and bring hope to those who didn't know the Lord. He was encouraging them to live consistently with what they said they believed.

To be honest, I'm struggling to learn this lesson myself. Even though we may not be suffering from persecution the way our brothers and sisters did in the past, you can't tell me we don't live in a world that needs hope! So we truly need to be prepared and encouraged to share our faith. In many nations of the world today, Christians are suffering severe persecution. And I believe that the day will come for the United States when persecution of Christians will intensify beyond just the social rejection of our beliefs that we experience today.

Second, *why* did Peter write his letter? For the same reason that I am writing: I want to both challenge you and encourage you. I'm a fellow pilgrim on this journey of faith. When it comes to me being bold in sharing the gospel, I've found that I'm like water; I'll take the path of least resistance and settle at the lowest level possible. I need someone to "squish" me out of my complacency. You might be surprised to find that it's not my natural tendency to be outgoing. Because of that, I've tried to surround myself with folks who I know will encourage me and challenge me to be more outspoken in my witness. I want to be "bold to speak the word without fear," like Paul, "knowing that I am appointed for the defense of the gospel" (Philippians 1:17). If you know Christ as your Savior, He's appointed you too!

Now, let's break down this verse and see if we can glean some nuggets to apply to our daily lives as followers of Christ. To learn how we can accomplish this challenging task of being ready with reasons and answers, we're going to look at three points Peter addresses in this verse to see how they apply to us. We'll consider the same two questions—*who* and *why*—and then address the challenge of *how*.

WHO DO WE SHARE WITH?

First, according to verse 15, *to whom* are we supposed to give a reason for our hope? "To every man that asketh you" (KJV).

Wow! According to God, we, as His children, should be ready and spiritually equipped to give an answer to *every* person who asks us about our faith. That includes both believers and nonbelievers. Yes, there are believers who have spiritual questions that need to be answered. (By the way, you're reading a book by one of them!) It also does not mean we are to wait for someone to ask us a question. The rest of Scripture makes it very clear that we are to be engaging the culture for Christ.

In addition, this world is full of lost people who don't know Jesus Christ as their Lord and Savior. They need to hear the truth, and God has called each of us to leave our comfort zone and get outside our "Christian bubble" by engaging these people and telling them how they can have hope.

In Matthew 16:15, Jesus asked His disciples, "But who do you say that I am?" Peter made his magnificent confession: "You are the Christ, the Son of the living God" (verse 16). Praise God for his bold answer! But let's backtrack a little bit and focus on the first question that Jesus asked His disciples in this passage, which appears at the end of verse 13. Jesus asked a slightly different question: "Who do *men* say that I, the Son of Man, am?" (emphasis added).

Do you understand the implications of those words? Through that simple question, Jesus revealed that He knew men were talking about Him and trying to figure out what He, the Messiah, was all about. Jesus' question also showed that *He expected His followers to be involved in active dialogue in the marketplace of ideas*, talking with people about spiritual issues.

Let me ask you this: how can we know what men and women think of Jesus unless we are engaged in a spiritual dialogue with them? God makes it very clear that we need to be focused on doing His business, not only in the church, but in the world around us as well.

Now, you may be saying to yourself, "That's a tall order. I can't do that. I'm not that smart. I'm not that qualified. I don't have a Ph.D. or a seminary degree. Going out and witnessing isn't my gift!" Trust me, I've heard all these excuses and more because I've used them myself.

Here is the cool thing: God doesn't rely on our wisdom, education, or giftedness to accomplish His work. The Lord doesn't care if we possess great genius or remarkable talents. After all, Jesus' disciples, for the most part, were ordinary, hardworking men. Most of the disciples were as "blue collar" as they come, but they knew Jesus, and their hearts burned with a passionate desire to share His truth with the world. And the Holy Spirit worked through them to spread the good news, lighting up the sin-darkened nations of the ancient world with the radiance of the gospel message.

The Lord allows us to go along for the ride as He accomplishes His works and His will through us (Philippians 2:13). All we have to do is follow Him, like the disciples did, and be humble and obedient to His call. Thankfully, we're not alone in our journey of faith. God has promised that when we trust in Jesus Christ, and His death on the cross that paid the penalty for our sins, then God saves us and the Holy Spirit will dwell within us. The Holy Spirit serves as our Comforter and Guide, providing conviction and wisdom to every person who has a true relationship with Jesus Christ. It's amazing what the Lord can do through us when we humbly say, "Here am I! Send me" (Isaiah 6:8).

WHY SHOULD WE SHARE?

Now, let's go to the next question that Peter answers in 1 Peter 3:15. *Why* are we supposed to be able to give a reason for our hope? Easy: God wants us to give a reason for our faith so that we can pass along our hope to those without hope. And God not only desires that we give a reason, He has *commanded* us to do so (Matthew 28:19; Mark 16:15; John 20:21; Acts 1:8). So the "why" is simple: because God said so. That settles it. As we explored in the previous chapter, *everyone* needs to know the only source of true hope—for this life and for the next. Consider this: Where would you spend eternity if someone had not explained the gospel to you?

When your heart is filled with gratitude for the salvation you've been given, it will spill out in love and compassion for others, so they too can know the "hope of salvation" (1 Thessalonians 5:8). To make sure your motive is right as you share your faith, ask yourself, "Am I doing this for the right reasons?" God cares as much about *why* we do what we do as *what* we do. You can feed and clothe all the poor in the world, but unless you've done it out of love for the Lord and for the lost, you've done it for the wrong reason, and there will be no crown waiting for you in heaven.

HOW DO WE SHARE?

Well, that still leaves the question, "How?" *How* are we going to accomplish our goal of being able to give a reason for our hope? Although God has promised to be with us and guide us, I don't want to imply that you and I don't have to do our part to be prepared to reach those in the world who don't know the Lord. The point of this book is that we *do* need to be prepared. God will do the work, but we are required to "study to show thyself approved unto God, a workman that needeth not to be ashamed, rightly dividing the word of truth" (2 Timothy 2:15, KJV).

You heard that right: we have to "study." The word also means to be "diligent" or "earnest." We have to do our part in being prepared for what the Lord is calling us to do. But make no mistake about it, God is the One who does the work and gets the glory.

Another question is, "How are we supposed to give these answers?" I discovered something interesting as I studied this verse. For years in my own life and ministry, I emphasized that we should "be ready always to give an answer," but I left out the end of the verse. And I missed an important clue that reveals something very close to the heart of God.

Here's what the whole verse says:

Chapter 3

But sanctify the Lord God in your hearts: and be ready always to give an answer to every man that asketh you a reason of the hope that is in you *with meekness and fear* (KJV, emphasis added)

Peter says we are to do this "with meekness and fear." Other translations say "with gentleness and reverence" (NASB), "with gentleness and respect" (NIV), or "courteously and respectfully" (Amplified). So before you open your mouth to share the gospel (or your testimony) with someone, ask yourself, "Am I doing this with meekness and fear? Am I responding with gentleness and respect?"

Unfortunately, in the past many of us involved in apologetics have focused on just the first part of the verse. Like me, you may have tried to "argue" people into the kingdom of heaven, which is rarely effective. (Trust me; I've tried many times to put someone in a spiritual full-nelson or chokehold, but it just doesn't work!) In Ephesians 4:15, Paul stressed the importance of "speaking the truth in love" especially when we are delicately trying to help people see their need for the Savior. Whenever you share the good news, ask yourself, "Am I doing this in a loving way?" We must represent Christ in kindness, gentleness, and love.

Now let's examine 1 Peter 3:16 to see what additional instructions Peter has for us regarding apologetics. He says that we should give a defense of our faith:

...having a good conscience; that, whereas they speak evil of you, as of evildoers, they may be ashamed that falsely accuse your good conversation in Christ. (KJV)

When we give answers for our faith, we will face scoffers and be reviled and criticized, so we should be prepared for it and not let the scoffers stop us from doing what God has commanded. But when we share our faith, we need to make sure our conduct doesn't give people any reason to doubt the truth of what we're saying. The gospel message is offensive enough; we don't want our behavior to be offensive too. Make sure you are blameless and act in good conscience, so that any accusations against you will be false. In 1 Peter 3:17 we are told, "For it is better, if it is the will of God, to suffer for doing good than for doing evil." And always trust that God will give you the strength to be bold and withstand persecution.

I can hear you saying, "Okay, we're done! It's officially impossible to accomplish all of these things in this manner!" Guess what? I agree. In our own strength, it is impossible for us to accomplish all of this. But the Bible reminds us that with God, all things are possible (Matthew 19:26; Mark 10:27).

My friend, please don't think you have to be a rocket scientist to share the gospel. You don't need a seminary degree or a high I.Q. to be able to give an answer about the reason for the hope within you. No matter your background, I believe you'll find this book to be an easy read and, more important, highly practical as I show you how you can use the rocky areas in your life as steppingstones for sharing the love of Christ with others.

So while the Lord may not be calling you to become a scholar in defending the Bible, He does command one thing: obedience in proclaiming His Word. It's humbling to realize that He will use you and me right where we are. All of us have neighbors, friends, colleagues, and family members who need Christ. God will work through our strengths and our weaknesses, as well as through whatever knowledge and skills we may or may not have. He is not concerned about what and who we *think* we are, but rather what and who *He says* we are in Christ. If we lack knowledge or confidence, God will make up for our weakness with His wisdom, power, and strength.

Telling Others How Jesus Has Changed Your Life

W hen I first became involved with ministry, I had the privilege of volunteering at a conference in Canada and it was an experience I will always remember. The conference was held at a beautiful facility, in a beautiful part of the world.

The woman who had worked hard to make this conference happen suffered from Multiple Sclerosis (MS) and walked with a cane. She had been totally bedridden for a few months prior to the event, so she was thanking God that she was able to attend the meetings. She'd been working on this event for almost a year and without God's help would not have been able to attend!

Our ministry team arrived early to meet with the team from the church and begin setup. We immediately encountered a struggle when what we needed to do wasn't what the church representative wanted to do, and a couple of the individuals started to argue. It caught me off guard and I remember sitting down and praying while these two "discussed" what was going to take place.

One thing Masami and I have learned over the years from such events is that, when everything around you starts going crazy and you don't understand what's going on, *be still, be patient, and wait on the Lord*. God is about to do something amazing! Satan will pull out all the stops to get you out of focus, so that you lose sight of what's really important.

Once that "discussion" was settled, we got busy and did what we had to do to make everything work. When the conference began the church was full and the responses were very good. After one of the speakers finished, three young ladies approached him and began asking numerous questions, so we went to another room and continued the conversation. The questions really came from only one young lady, named Natasha. The speaker did a truly amazing job of answering her questions, and it was such a blessing to watch and learn from this encounter.

After about twenty minutes of questions the real issue finally came out. Natasha said, "You don't understand—God could never forgive me. You have no idea the things that I've done!" She explained that her parents belonged to a cult and shared some of the truly terrible things that had been done to her. As she spoke Natasha never looked us in the eyes, but had her head down, looking at the ground.

After she shared this, the speaker pointed toward me and said, "Natasha, God can forgive you. You don't know how bad *he* was!" Then he looked at me and said, "Tell her your story, Carl." What an honor it was to share some of the "boulders" in my life that you'll read about in this book, and to show this young lady what an amazing God we serve. As I truly just poured my heart out to her, she started shaking and looked as if she was going to pass out. We quickly grabbed a chair and sat her down. I then shared the gospel with her and asked if she wanted to trust Christ as her personal Savior. She said yes!

In that small room, beside the sanctuary, I was able to proclaim the gospel to Natasha and she prayed for Jesus to save her. Praise the Lord! When I saw Natasha the next day she was a different person. She exuded *hope* and joy. She looked me in the eyes and was truly a beautiful sight to behold. She was a new creation in Christ and His light shone brightly through her.

At the end of the conference, a gentleman from the church thanked those who attended and recognized the people who had made the event happen. As he asked the woman with MS to come forward and share a few words, this dear lady was mortified! She was a humble saint, seeking no recognition, but now she had to go in front of people and say something! I watched as she struggled down the aisle and up the stairs. You could see the fear on her face as she stood before the group. She opened her mouth and said, "Praise be to God, great things He hath done!" And she walked off the stage and back down the aisle.

There are two points that have stayed with me ever since that first ministry trip. First, that humble servant of the Lord, who had just pulled off a *very* successful conference in a *very* difficult environment, gave all the glory to God!

Second, because Natasha's "strongholds" were broken down, she was able to hear the gospel message that I shared with her, understand her need for a Savior, confess her sins, and open her heart to the saving grace of the Lord.

I was nothing more than a "roadie," setting up books and doing grunt work. But I was also a minister of the gospel of Jesus Christ. Please hear me when I say, we are *all* ministers of the gospel of Jesus Christ! Don't let the opportunities He gives you to share your faith pass you by. Share those broken pieces of your life with someone when given the opportunity and point them to Christ, to what He has done through those experiences and in your life.

"ONE THING I KNOW"

Here's another example of an individual's personal testimony. I love the biblical story of the blind man whom Jesus healed, recorded by the disciple John in chapter 9 of his Gospel. People kept asking the man questions, but he always responded by simply telling them how Jesus had transformed his life. The Jews, however, just couldn't accept the fact that Jesus had healed this man. Here's the passage:

> Now as Jesus passed by, He saw a man who was blind from birth. And His disciples asked Him, saying, "Rabbi, who sinned, this man or his parents, that he was born blind?"
>
> Jesus answered, "Neither this man nor his parents sinned, but that the works of God should be revealed in him. I must work the works of Him who sent Me while it is day; the night is coming when no one can work. As long as I am in the world, I am the light of the world."
>
> When He had said these things, He spat on the ground and made clay with the saliva; and He anointed the eyes of the blind man with the clay. And He said to him, "Go, wash in the pool of Siloam" (which is translated, Sent). So he went and washed, and came back seeing.
>
> Therefore the neighbors and those who previously had seen that he was blind said, "Is not this he who sat and begged?"
>
> Some said, "This is he." Others said, "He is like him." He said, "I am he."
>
> Therefore they said to him, "How were your eyes opened?"
>
> He answered and said, "A Man called Jesus made clay and anointed my eyes and said to me, 'Go to the pool of Siloam and wash.' So I went and washed, and I received sight." (John 9:1–11)

Chapter 4

The Pharisees didn't like this scene one bit, especially because the day on which Jesus had made the mud and opened the man's eyes was a Sabbath. It amazes me that people can get so "religious" that they're more concerned about the day of the week on which a miracle happened than the fact that a miracle just happened! John continues:

Therefore some of the Pharisees said, "This Man is not from God, because He does not keep the Sabbath."

Others said, "How can a man who is a sinner do such signs?" And there was a division among them.

They said to the blind man again, "What do you say about Him because He opened your eyes?"

He said, "He is a prophet."

But the Jews did not believe concerning him, that he had been blind and received his sight, until they called the parents of him who had received his sight. And they asked them, saying, "Is this your son, who you say was born blind? How then does he now see?"

His parents answered them and said, "We know that this is our son, and that he was born blind; but by what means he now sees we do not know, or who opened his eyes we do not know. He is of age; ask him. He will speak for himself." His parents said these things because they feared the Jews, for the Jews had agreed already that if anyone confessed that He was Christ, he would be put out of the synagogue. Therefore his parents said, "He is of age; ask him."

So they again called the man who was blind, and said to him, "Give God the glory! We know that this Man is a sinner."

He answered and said, "Whether He is a sinner or not I do not know. One thing I know: that though I was blind, now I see." (John 9:16–25)

The religious folks kept questioning the man. They were trying to corner him, giving him and his parents an opportunity to "play ball" with the world. Notice that the man's parents didn't say that Jesus had healed their son because they were afraid of the religious leaders. These leaders could have had the parents barred from the synagogue for suggesting that Jesus was the Messiah.

The Pharisees commanded the healed man: "Give God the glory! We know that this Man [Jesus] is a sinner." Kick Jesus to the curb, so to speak, and everything would be okay! But verse 25 is such a comfort to a weak, fallible individual like me. The blind man, who had been healed by the Son of God, makes this incredible statement: "Whether He is a sinner or not I do not know. *One thing I know: that though I was blind, now I see.*"

I feel like that so often when people ask me spiritual and biblical questions. Even though I study the Scriptures and try my best to be "rightly dividing the word of truth" (2 Timothy 2:15), there's still so much about the Bible and the Christian life that I don't know. When someone asks me a question and I am not sure of the answer, I try to remember to say, "To be honest, I don't know the answer to that question, but hey, *I know this!* Let me share with you what Jesus has done in my life."

Sharing our stories of life change doesn't have to be formal or dramatic. Sometimes a simple truth can make all the difference. I use this approach because I know that I am not God, and I don't know everything. But in addition to telling what Jesus has done for me, when someone asks a question that I don't know the answer to, I'll either point the person to where he can find the answer, or I'll offer to research the topic myself and then get back to him. I believe that's my calling because of what God has commanded us to do in 1 Peter.

When I contact people after I have found the answer to their question, they typically respond with surprise and disbelief. Trust me: if you make the effort to get back to people with answers to their questions, they will be shocked and impressed, and they will be motivated to listen to you. Why? Because very few Christians bother to do the research and then follow through!

When you make a promise to find an answer for people, and you keep that promise, those people will realize that you truly care about them and their souls. They'll know that you are interested in their questions, and you have a heart that longs for their salvation, or, if they are already saved, you desire that they grow in their knowledge of the Lord and His Word.

I think you will discover as you read through this book that the Bible gives us answers—often easy-to-understand answers—that help us declare and defend our Christian faith even in these challenging, anti-Christian times. I'm sure you've noticed that we live in an age when God, the Bible, and biblical principles are constantly under attack. Only by being honest, prepared, and obedient will we be able to give the reasons for our hope.

I trust you'll get excited about your faith as you receive answers concerning the Bible's trustworthiness and see how relevant the Scriptures are for us today. And, I'm excited about sharing with you my own personal odyssey that led me to become a Christian and then enabled me to get involved in a dynamic ministry that God has used to change countless lives.

LIVING STONES

We talked earlier about how the Israelites used stones to build memorials after they had crossed the Jordan River on dry ground. These stones served as a testimony to future generations of what the Lord had done for them as they entered the Promised Land.

As Christ-followers, all of us are "living stones" whose lives are built upon the chief Cornerstone, Jesus. We are stones of testimony, displaying God's handiwork. We read in 1 Peter 2:4–7:

> Coming to Him as to a living stone, rejected indeed by men, but chosen by God and precious, you also, as living stones, are being built up a spiritual house, a holy priesthood, to offer up spiritual sacrifices acceptable to God through Jesus Christ. Therefore it is also contained in the Scripture,
>
> > "Behold, I lay in Zion
> > A chief cornerstone, elect, precious,
> > And he who believes on Him will by no means be
> > put to shame."
>
> Therefore, to you who believe, He is precious; but to those who are disobedient,
>
> > "The stone which the builders rejected [Jesus]
> > Has become the chief cornerstone"...

As you read through Part 2 of this book, you'll learn about some large obstacles—boulders, really—that became major hurdles in my life. But I'll share with you how God, in His grace, removed these stumbling stones and set my feet on the solid Rock of Jesus Christ. As a result, I became a living stone in His house.

I hope my story will challenge you to start thinking about the boulders and obstacles that God has helped you overcome in your life and then share them with a generation that is asking, "What do these stones mean?" You don't have to know everything—but you can tell people what Jesus has done for you and how He has changed your life. By being obedient to what God calls us to do, we'll be equipped to offer reasons for our hope to a dry and thirsty world.

PART TWO

MY STORY:

*From Wrestler's Son
to Professional Speaker*

Life as the Son of a Professional Wrestler

I t would be quite an understatement for me to say that I grew up in a very unusual household. My father was a professional wrestler who went by the name "Luke 'Big Boy' Brown."

I like to joke with my seminar audiences about what it was like to grow up around guys with one-word names like Crusher, Bruiser, Mauler, and Assassin. When you're spending time with guys with names like these, trust me—I.Q. and academic achievement aren't stressed!

Growing up I was the oldest of five children. When I was a young, my mom took our family to church on a pretty regular basis, but I didn't understand what it meant to be a born-again Christian. Back then, I had no idea that a person could establish a saving, personal relationship with God through Christ. My parents had set some rules and regulations for us to follow at home, but I didn't know what the Bible said about how we should live our lives. In fact, at the liberal churches we attended, the subject of the accuracy of the Bible and how it applied to the world we lived in was never addressed.

My father (left) vs. the "Bruiser"

Because my father traveled so much, I don't remember him going to church with us very often. But I do remember one occasion when he sat in the pew, sleeping. He was 6'8", weighed 350 pounds, and snored like a freight train, so it wasn't a pretty sight! Dad could sleep anywhere, though.

I also remember my mom taking me to church for catechism classes. I wasn't too thrilled about having to take those classes, but there was no question about it, I had to attend. They took place after school, so Mom would drop me off at church and leave until I was finished. I'd walk in the front door—then hang a left and head out the side door and off to the playground! Mom never saw where I went once the door closed behind me. Then, right before she arrived to pick me up, I would return through the side door and walk out the front as if I had been in class the whole time. (And she never knew about it until this confession. Sorry, Mom!)

A few years ago, I found the actual book that I had been given for these classes. As I thumbed through it, I noticed that the only indication the book had ever been opened was my name written on the first page. That's it; I hadn't even opened the rest of the book. Yet you know what? The church gave me a passing mark in catechism! Isn't that sad?

Christians, we can't just pass somebody along like that. I hadn't learned a thing about the Bible! We've got to take belief in the Bible seriously, and be intentional about passing on that legacy to the next generation. Those in spiritual leadership, especially, should not just go through the motions and give people a false sense of spiritual security. The Lord wants more for us than that.

LONELY HOURS

Yes, life with a professional wrestler for a father could be really strange—and for more than just the obvious reasons. Our family went from one extreme to another; we had times when we could afford to live in a very nice house, and we faced times of severe need and financial hardship.

At one point, we lived in Elkton, Maryland, in a trailer, and we needed more space. To "solve the problem," my dad bought another trailer—an inexpensive one that had been flood-damaged. It had mud caked on the walls about three feet high where water and dirt had swept through the trailer. I'll never forget the horrible, musty smell of mold and mildew that filled that place. To connect the two trailers, my father simply used a buzz saw to cut a large hole in the side of each trailer, then he built a walkway between the two using plywood. And that's what we lived in. Dad was pretty practical!

As a child, I was told that my grandmother's house had been built from used orange crates. It eventually burned down because rats chewed on the electrical wires, sparking a fire. And when I say rats, I do mean rats—big ones!

One night before the house burned down, I remember sitting at the kitchen table playing cards with my family. My grandmother had placed a large rat trap—one of those old quarter-inch-thick wooden traps, not a small mousetrap—in the laundry room. I heard the trap go off and went to see what it had caught. What I saw was a "monster" rat—the biggest one I had ever seen. It was so big that even the large trap didn't kill it. I watched in horror as this huge rat flopped around the laundry room floor while caught in the trap. Eventually my grandmother had to come and kill the rat herself! I wasn't getting close to that monster.

I recently asked my mother to share with me some of her memories of my childhood. Here's what she told me:

When I got pregnant with you, we were living in California. Dennis [my dad] decided to go visit his family in Maryland. We went through Kentucky to visit his sister Ann en route to Maryland.

After about a week, we went to Maryland for what I thought was a visit. The first night we were there, I was scared, feeling like I had walked into some kind of bad movie. Everybody was sitting around the table in the kitchen, some on chairs and the rest on lard cans. All of them were drinking tea out of quart canning jars—they didn't even have real drinking glasses. But I did okay until a chicken strolled into the kitchen and everybody started yelling to shoo it out. I passed out! I woke up looking up at his mom leaning over me. I wanted to run away, but there was no place to go.

I really thought it was a visit; I didn't realize that we would be moving to Maryland then. Dennis stayed for a while, but soon he left me there and went to Toronto, Canada, to hook up with his old friend, Frank Townsend. He was quite successful wrestling there. Throughout the rest of my pregnancy, I didn't see him at all until the week I was due.

Chapter 5

Dennis did call me once a week, though. Since it was the home phone, he spoke to everybody in the family, so our conversations usually were very short. When my due date was close, he came home for a couple of days. I went into labor the day he had to leave to go back to Canada, so he stayed only long enough to drive me to the hospital.

I knew he would not stay with me at the hospital, and I don't think I have ever been that scared in my life. I was only eighteen years old, and I wanted my mom! But Dennis just dropped me off at the hospital and drove back up to Canada. His mom said he called every little while en route to his match that night.

After you were born, my mother-in-law told Dennis that I had finally had a boy weighing seven pounds and four ounces. He went back and had it announced on TV that his wife had just given birth to a nine-pound baby boy!

The next time I saw him was when you were a month old. He came and got me and we moved to Hamilton, Ontario, to a place called The Pig and Whistle Inn. It was a bar with some cabins behind it. Dennis fell right through the front porch of the first cabin we moved into, so the owners moved us into another cabin. The legs of the bed fell through the floor, but we actually stayed in that one. I kept the bottles of milk for you in the bathtub with cold water running over them because we had no fridge. We just had an icebox, and we got ice once a week.

Dennis traveled a lot, so you and I stayed in the cabin by ourselves most of the time. My brother Dale came up to visit once. He killed the big rat that had been crawling out of the wall and terrorizing me all the time.

Those are my memories of Canada. When your dad was close by, he would take us to the matches with him, but that didn't happen very often.

We had a French-Canadian neighbor lady who used to put both your feet in one of her hands and dance you around while she sang a French song. Several of us women would sit out in the yard and play Pokeno, I believe it was called. It was like bingo with playing cards. It filled lots of lonely hours.

I do remember one time when you were about eight months old. We had traveled back down south somewhere, probably to North or South Carolina, for one of your dad's wrestling matches. I wanted to go to the arena with him, but he insisted that we could not go that night. He rented a room for us to stay in while he went to the arena. I will never forget the name: The Polka Dot Inn. It was filthy!

Dennis told the guy at the desk to bring a crib for you. He brought in an old, beat-up Porta-crib with a

My mother and father

dirty blanket on it that was supposed to be used as a mattress. I refused to put you into that filthy crib. I held you in my arms and sat on the only wooden chair in the room all night until your dad came back for us. That was one of the longest nights of my life.

The bedspread on the bed in that room was nasty, and the pillows were dirty. It was very clear that place had not been cleaned in a long time. After the match, your father came back and laid down and slept for two or three hours before we could leave to drive home. You and I stayed on the wooden chair so I could be sure that nothing was going to crawl on us!

In spite of all of this, that period of my life was not unhappy all the time. I was very much in love with your dad.

My mom's account of the early years of my life shows that she encountered some challenging "boulders," too. She persevered, but she faced some tough circumstances during that time. I think you'll agree that it's difficult to glorify the life of a professional wrestler when you hear stories like these.

Without Christ in their lives making a husband and wife truly "one flesh," a lifestyle like this can destroy a marriage. Love alone was not enough and my parents ended up divorcing when I was thirteen years old. But, praise God, my mom is now in a position where she can minister to people. God has prepared her to offer hope to those who are dealing with the same issues and don't know there is another way.

MILITARY BOUND

A short time later my mother remarried and my stepfather began attending law school in Lexington, Virginia. I was around fourteen when our family moved there.

I started attending Lexington High School as a freshman, and things went pretty well until my senior year. That was another one of those turning points in my life when God really looked out for me in spite of myself.

That year, my stepfather graduated from law school and took a job in northern Virginia. This meant we had to move again, but I decided I wanted nothing to do with that. I had moved my entire life, and now that I was going into my last year of school I didn't want to have to pick up and start over again somewhere else. So, rather than moving, I asked to stay in Lexington with Don and Nancy Leech, the neighbors who rented us a home next to theirs. They were a Christian family and dear people. Don and Nancy were kind enough to open their home and allow me to stay with them. They truly modeled Christianity for me, and the time I spent with them has had a lasting impact on me. (Thank you, Don and Nancy, for putting up with me during that difficult time. I know I put more stress on you than all of your daughters combined!)

One of Don and Nancy's family rules was that if I lived with them, I had to attend church with their family. Not having much of a choice in the matter, I joined them in going to church. To be frank, the only thing in church at that time that appealed to me was this couple's daughter! Yes, I went to church with them, but believe me, I wasn't a Christian. The last half of my senior year, I used drugs and alcohol pretty much every day. I was out of control.

A few months before my high school graduation, my life had spiraled so out of control with the drugs and alcohol that I moved out of Don and Nancy's home and into an apartment with some cadets from the Virginia Military Institute (VMI). Why would I do that? Why would I leave a family that really blessed me and took great care of me? I was an idiot, to put it bluntly. I didn't want anyone telling me what to do, and in many ways I was embarrassed—I knew what I was doing was wrong, and being around Don and Nancy just reinforced the guilt I felt. So instead of dealing with the issue, I ran away from it. My life quickly went downhill from there. Without the stabilizing influence of godly people like Don and Nancy in my life, I ran headlong into a life of sin.

Near the end of my senior year, I threw a book at my English teacher. I never did care for school, as you can probably tell. The only thing that kept me in school was sports. The problem was that the drugs and alcohol interfered with my athletic performance as well as my academic performance. Due to my substance abuse, I ended up getting kicked off the basketball team. That broke my heart because I really did love basketball.

Because I threw a book at my English teacher, I failed English. (I didn't know what the big deal was; I didn't hit her with it! It was just a warning shot to get her to stop making fun of me.) Because I failed the class, I had to attend summer school to finish English before I could receive my diploma. Summer school was held in a town a few miles away, so I had to drive there every day. After a few weeks, I ran out of time, interest, and money, so I quit summer school and didn't get my high school diploma.

I continued my downward spiral, traveling down the wrong path. By then, I had no job, no future, and no plans. In fact, I didn't even have a home anymore. I had lost the apartment I'd lived in with the VMI cadets once school was out of session.

While I was homeless, I ended up sleeping on a couch in the girl's restroom at VMI when school wasn't in session. (At that time VMI didn't have any female students, but they had a girl's restroom for visitors. It was not often used, and since the window had been left open, I just crawled in and slept there. Hey, the price was right!)

Lacking any other options at that point, I decided to join the military. I went down to the Army recruiting office in Lexington, signed up, and took the entrance test many miles away in Richmond. The guy sitting next to me during the exam couldn't read at all. Believe it or not, the sergeant who was monitoring the test walked up to the poor guy and helped him fill out the test!

That concerned me. While I didn't have a high school diploma myself, I was worried about the prospect of spending a lot of time in the military with folks who couldn't even read—clearly, guys who were a whole lot worse off than I was. I was trying to get myself out of a bad situation, not get myself into a worse one!

During the evaluation process, the recruiters discovered that I was five pounds overweight for the Army. I was shocked! If you look at me today, you'd say, "Of course you're over-weight!" But in high school, that just wasn't the case. I lived to play sports, and I was in excellent physical shape. I couldn't believe this was happening. I thought, *How bad is this? Now I can't even join the military! What's going on?*

In desperation, I told the recruiter, "Give me an hour or so; I can lose five pounds of water weight pretty quickly." But he said that wasn't legal; I had to wait at least a week before I could be weighed again.

I was absolutely devastated. I didn't have anyone or anything to go back to. I had lost my job at a local greenhouse. I had lost my apartment. I had severed my relationships with many of the people I cared about. To their credit, the Leeches probably would have allowed me to move back in with them (that's just the kind of people they are), but I had wrecked their car while driving drunk and although they *never* said anything to me, I was too embarrassed to go back to them. Proverbs 28:1 sure makes sense to me: "The wicked flee when no one pursues." I was stuck in sin and just didn't think rationally! I had nowhere to go, and I didn't know what to do.

Before I left to go back to Lexington, the recruiter called me into his office and shut the door. He then asked me a question that I heard many times over the next few years. (I can't even remember his name; I truly wish I could so I could thank him.) With my test papers in front of him, the recruiter looked me right in the eyes and said, "What're you doing?"

His gaze seared straight through me. I didn't know what he was getting at. "What do you mean?" I replied.

He asked, "Why do you want to come into the Army?"

"To be honest," I told him, "I don't have a whole lot going on in my life. I don't have a job. I don't have a place to live. I really don't have anything." I didn't tell him, but it was at this time that I was sneaking in and sleeping in the girls' bathroom at VMI.

"Well," this Army recruiter told me, "don't enter the Army." I was stunned. Here was the man responsible for getting young men and women to join the Army, and he was telling me that I shouldn't join?

"You'd go nuts after a month. Your test scores are too high," he told me. In fact, he went on to explain that many of the Army training manuals were written and illustrated in a comic book style so that the young enlistees (even those who couldn't read) could understand them.

"You can sleep on my couch until you find a job," he said.

Now, please don't think that I'm trying to disparage the U.S. Army or any branch of our military, because I'm not. I greatly respect the young men and women who so willingly and bravely serve our nation and keep us free. In fact, one of the highlights of my ministry occurred when I was given the privilege of addressing over two thousand Marine recruits in basic training. Things have changed quite drastically in our military over the last thirty years, but I'm just sharing what happened to me.

The truth was, I didn't see much prospect in finding another job. So I told the recruiter, "I really need to get into the military."

"Well, if you're going to go into the military, go in the Air Force," he said. So, believe it or not, this Army recruiter took my test scores and paperwork over to an Air Force recruiter, and the Air Force accepted me. I still had to go home for a week and lose those five pounds, though, so I left the recruiter's office and went back to Lexington with my tail between my legs, so to speak.

The sound of those iron bars clanging shut literally jarred me to my senses. The shock hit me full force when I realized: I was not in control of my life anymore.

Thankfully, when I returned to Lexington, the parents of one of my friends were kind enough to allow me to stay with them at their home. I'll never forget the kindness of these dear people. Every time I go to Lexington, I check in with them and let them know how grateful I am for their gracious hospitality. They accepted me as one of their own and treated me as if I were their son.

One night that week while waiting for the Air Force to allow me to enlist, I went partying. After drinking quite a bit, I was walking home at about two o'clock in the morning. I staggered down the middle of a Lexington side road that had no traffic at all, when I heard a voice holler, "Halt! Police!" Well, I didn't want to stop because I had a bottle of alcohol in my hand, so I just kept on walking. He yelled out again, "Halt! Police!"

I quickly walked over to the side of the road and discreetly tossed the bottle into the grass so he wouldn't catch me with it.

As the police officer walked up to me, I recognized him. He was a young man who was currently dating a girl I used to date, so I immediately knew I was in trouble. I was certain this young lady had not spoken very well of me. And sure enough, after an altercation, the cop arrested me and threw me in jail for the night.

That was the longest night of my life. I was in a cell with three other men. These guys were *not* ones anyone in Lexington would want to hang out with (but then neither was I that night)! Here I was in jail with them. The sound of those iron bars clanging shut literally jarred me to my senses. The shock hit me full force when I realized a sobering truth: *I was not in control of my life anymore.* There wasn't a thing I could do except sit there until morning.

The next day when I stood before a judge, he gave me a choice: either face the charges (drunkenness, disorderly conduct, and resisting arrest) or follow through with joining the military. Hmmm, join the military or go to jail? Tough decision, right? Needless to say, I chose the military option.

The judge put me on house arrest until I left for the military, so I had to remain in my friend's house for the next few days until I could go back to the recruitment center. The police drove by every so often to check on me.

My friend and I just waved to them from the front porch.

From a Jail Cell to a Control Tower

At the end of my week of house arrest, I took the bus back to the recruiting station, this time as an Air Force recruit, and took the physical again. Interestingly, for whatever reason, when I took the physical this time the maximum weight limitation had increased by 6 pounds! To this day, I honestly cannot tell you how that happened. When I had been there the week before, the maximum weight (which was based on my height and therefore should not have changed) was 205 pounds. I had weighed 210 pounds then, so I wasn't allowed to join. This time the max weight was 211 pounds. That week I weighed in at 201 pounds, so I made it into the Air Force with ten pounds to spare.

Now that I had passed the physical, the only thing left for me to do was pick a job from the positions available in the Air Force. I noticed that Security Police was one of the choices, so I requested that position so I could be a dog handler. I loved animals, and that sounded like an awesome job. But the recruiter told me that the quota of Security Police had already been filled for the month, so I would have to wait and come back the next month if I wanted that job.

In fact, the Air Force didn't have available *any* of the jobs that I was interested in because it was the end of the month, and all the good jobs had already been taken.

"I have to leave immediately," I told him. "What jobs do you have open?"

"All we have is administration," he said.

"I'll take it," I replied and left that day for basic training.

■ ■ ■

Basic training was relatively easy for me since I'd played sports for so long. Because I had always heard how tough it was, I actually had already been working out in preparation, so the physical training was no issue for me. My drill sergeant made me the PT (Physical Training) leader, and I enjoyed leading the exercise time.

While the physical demands weren't too difficult for me, I found the mental, emotional, and relational aspects of basic training to be an enormous challenge. I've always had a hard time keeping my mouth shut when I should, and I still struggle with that to this day. (Please know that I am far from perfect and I just praise God that I'm forgiven!)

During my rebellious teen years, I had developed a very sharp tongue and a low tolerance for authority. That was not a good combination for a serviceman.

The pressure of basic training combined with the challenges of living with people I didn't know brought this weakness to light, big time! I had a few verbal altercations with various individuals throughout my weeks of training. On one occasion, I asked the drill sergeant to put me in the Day Room with a certain individual with whom I had a disagreement, and give us ten minutes alone so we could "work things out."

The drill sergeant didn't do that, of course. Instead, he sat us down and made us talk and reason through our issues.

Sergeant Cross was my drill sergeant's name, and it was a fitting one, because he was "cross" all the time. But thankfully, despite the occasions when my mouth got me into trouble, I was able to finish my basic training.

Just before we prepared to leave for our new jobs, Sergeant Cross gathered all of us into the Day Room to give us a pep talk. He asked each of us to stand up and report who we were and what job we were going to train for. When he got to me, I stood up and said, "My name is Carl Kerby, and I'm going into administration."

For the first time in basic training, I heard Sergeant Cross laugh. He thought that was hilarious. It was not a "nice" laugh, either; he was shocked. I asked him, "What's wrong, sir?"

"A big guy like you, pounding on a typewriter all day? They're going to call you a ——!" he replied. I can't tell you what he called me; suffice it to say that it wasn't very flattering.

I told him that I didn't want to be called that name. "How can I get out of administration?" I asked.

He told me to go and volunteer for a new job at the CBPO, which was the Consolidated Base Personnel Office, now known as MPF or Military Personnel Flight. (Don't you just love acronyms? If you ever decide to go into the military, YB— you'd better!)

I took his advice and went to the CBPO where I was told they had three jobs that I could volunteer for:

1. EOD (Explosive Ordinance Disposal Specialist): *Yeah, right!* I thought. Call me what you want; I'm not messing with bombs!

2. PRT (Pararescue Team): This sounded really interesting. However, they wouldn't let me sign up for this job because I'd hurt my knee while playing football in high school. With that

type of injury, they told me that I couldn't complete the rigorous training that the paratroopers had to master, making me ineligible for PRT.

3. ATC (Air-Traffic Control): I asked the man, "What's Air-Traffic Control?" I genuinely had no idea what it was. I thought an air-traffic controller was the guy who stood out on the tarmac with earphones on, using big orange flashlights to direct planes toward the gates.

The sergeant replied, "In the wintertime you're in a heated room, and in the summertime you're in an air-conditioned room!" Sounded good to me. I accepted the position.

Back then, I didn't realize that God's hand was leading me and guiding me all the time. It may have seemed like happenstance that I ended up in the Air Force instead of the Army, and it may have seemed like chance that all the "good jobs" were taken, so I ended up in ATC. But, as a Christian, I now know that seemingly random acts actually are not random at all. God orchestrates every single one, and I believe He was assembling the pieces of my life for my good and His glory.

Our loving God is always watching over us, and even when we don't feel His presence or trust Him, He cares for us. The Bible says in Psalm 139:

O LORD, You have searched me and known me.
You know my sitting down and my rising up;
    You understand my thought afar off.
You comprehend my path and my lying down,
    And are acquainted with all my ways.
For there is not a word on my tongue,
    But behold, O LORD, You know it altogether.
You have hedged me behind and before,
    And laid Your hand upon me.
Such knowledge is too wonderful for me;
    It is high, I cannot attain it. (Psalm 139:1–6)

Chapter 6

When I am signing books at one of my speaking events, I always add this verse:

> "Fear not, for I am with you; be not dismayed, for I am your God. I will strengthen you, yes, I will help you, I will uphold you with My righteous right hand." (Isaiah 41:10)

Even when you and I don't see God's hand, He is still right there, upholding us. You can trust Him fully with your life. He will never let you fall!

MARRIAGE TO A "COMMUNIST" IN JAPAN

When I first became an air-traffic controller in the Air Force, getting married was the furthest thing from my mind. But God had a different plan for me.

Following basic training I was sent to Tech School where I learned to be an air-traffic controller. After finishing the school my first base assignment was Yokota Air Force Base (AFB) in Japan. Thankfully, I had already wanted to go to Japan because of all the positive things my father had told me about the country. He had wrestled there and brought back posters and photos of Japan. His accounts of the country intrigued me, so I was interested in seeing it.

In a most unusual way, the Lord opened the door for me to meet my future wife, Masami, while stationed in Japan. He also led me through a variety of circumstances that allowed me to learn what the Bible says about the responsibilities of being a husband and a father.

I had been stationed in Japan for about two years when I met Masami. Back then, I liked to go to a disco called Radio City. (Yes, a *disco!* You have to remember that this was back in the 1980s, during my B.C. [before Christ] days.) I liked that particular disco because you could eat and drink all you wanted for one price. For an airman on a fixed budget, that was a great deal, especially because I eat so much!

原始人の背骨を砕くG馬場の波乗り地獄!

My father on tour in Japan, wrestling Giant Baba

One night, I went to Radio City with a girl, and I saw Masami on the dance floor. I wasn't all that interested in the girl I was with, so I went out on the dance floor and danced with Masami. (I was not a very nice guy!) Masami was there with a group of girlfriends from her work. We enjoyed dancing and talking a bit, so we set up a day to meet at the club the following week.

The next time we met at Radio City, Masami had five of her friends with her. That's not what I expected to happen! But we hit it off and started dating after that. We had a very short relationship before getting engaged. In fact, we were married within six months of the day we met!

Masami, like most Japanese, was not a Christian at that time, and as I mentioned, neither was I.

When we decided to get married, the U.S. military had to do a background check on Masami. We submitted the necessary paperwork, but the military did not get back to us for quite a while. Something was up. We were now about a month away from the wedding, I went to the military office to inquire about the long delay. I was told to step into a back room.

In the windowless room filled with locked filing cabinets, a military official unlocked one of the drawers and pulled out a folder. He looked me in the eyes and declared, "You can't marry this girl."

Stunned, I asked, "What do you mean, I can't marry her?"

"You can't," he replied. "She's a communist."

The man proceeded to explain to me why they thought Masami was a communist. In the paperwork she had filled for her background search, one section of a form asked about about all the organizations and groups that she belonged to. One group Masami was a member of was Minsei, the union at the "Christian" orphanage where she worked. Apparently, Minsei was a socialist-based organization, and Masami was very active in the union. For example, she'd written letters to the Japanese government stating that she was against the use of nuclear weapons. Because of this, the American government (and the military) had classified Masami as a "communist."

"You can't marry her," the officer informed me. "And if you do, she'll never be able to immigrate to the United States."

Incredulous, I told the officer, "That just doesn't make any sense to me. Hello?! We're in *Japan!* Of course, people here are against nuclear weapons. We melted thousands of people here in WWII. And if being against nuclear weapons makes you a communist, then color me red—I'm against using nuclear weapons." Smart-mouth Carl strikes again!

"Well, the Air Force can't force you not to marry her, but she'll never be allowed to live in America because the computer says she's a communist," he replied.

We decided to get married anyway.

NEXT STOP: THE AZORES ISLANDS

Two years after Masami and I were married, the Air Force transferred us from Japan to the Azores Islands, located in the Atlantic Ocean west of Portugal. The U.S. Air Force had a strategic base there.

Masami had brought a Bible with her to the Azores as part of her plan to be able to immigrate to America. Her idea was that if any immigration or military official told her that she couldn't enter America because she was a communist, she was going to pull out her Bible and declare, "I'm not a communist; I'm a Christian. Look, here's my Bible!"

Well, that wasn't a very solid plan. Fortunately, the Lord had a much better plan for us. You see, when we arrived in the Azores, there was nothing for Masami to do. There was no Japanese television, no Japanese magazines—no Japanese any-thing. In fact, there was no *English* television, either! But Masami had her Bible. So she began reading the Word of God.

Believe it or not, there were only five Japanese people on the entire island—that's it! Five ladies. But all of them just *happened* to be Christians. These women started sharing their faith with Masami, and she had many questions for them. In response they challenged her to keep reading the Bible, and she did. In addition, there was an American missionary, Pastor Albert Hill and his wife, who lived on the island, and he also answered many of Masami's questions.

Amazingly, one of the first questions Masami asked these Christians was, "How do dinosaurs fit in with the teachings of the Bible?" I didn't know this until many years after the fact. Sadly, none of those ladies nor the missionary could answer that question. It's fascinating to me that this was the very ques-tion that got me so excited years later when someone gave me a biblical answer—and that answer led to me getting involved in creation ministry!

During this time of her spiritual searching, Masami and I began to experience marital problems. I remember coming home one day and telling her, "You know what? You need to go to church. I stayed with a family back in Virginia, and they were Christians. They didn't have problems in their marriage. *You* need to go to church." I considered myself a Christian already. I'd been baptized, and I had grown up in America. Of course I was a Christian, right? But how wrong I was.

Thankfully, despite my preachy attitude, Masami was open to my suggestion. She had been reading her Bible, and she believed that both of us attending church would help us to overcome our marital issues.

The Word of God addresses how to handle all kinds of different issues in every area of life. It teaches us so much about how to develop godly relationships between husbands and wives, parents and children. It teaches that life is not about us and our interests, but about God and His plan. As she continued to read the Scriptures, Masami began to apply biblical principles to our marriage and family relationships.

I didn't know it yet, but due to what she had read in God's Word, Masami had already surrendered her heart to Jesus Christ. She knew she was a sinner, and she had repented on her own while sitting at a small table in our kitchen. So, when we went to church on that particular Sunday morning and the pastor gave an invitation to come forward, Masami did so to show her obedience.

Once she was born again, I could see an obvious change in her as she continued to read the Word more and as she sought to become a godly wife. As a result, she and I had fewer arguments and problems at home.

I'm constantly amazed at how lives can be radically transformed by the Word of God. Hebrews 4:12 says, "For the word of God is living and powerful, and sharper than any two-edged sword, piercing even to the division of soul and spirit, and of joints and marrow, and is a discerner of the thoughts and intents of the heart." As I saw Masami grow and mature in her faith, I started to rethink my own attitudes and actions.

Many of the world's foremost leaders, writers, and thinkers have described how transformational the Word of God has been in their lives. One of our nation's greatest presidents, Abraham Lincoln, wrote, "I believe the Bible is the best gift God has ever given to man. All the good from the Savior of the world is communicated to us through this book."

Our nation's first president, George Washington, said, "It is impossible to rightly govern the world without God and the Bible."

Even the philosopher Immanuel Kant wrote, "The existence of the Bible, as a book for the people, is the greatest benefit which the human race has ever experienced. Every attempt to belittle it is a crime against humanity."

Alexander Campbell, a pastor and leader in the Second Great Awakening in America, said, "The Bible is to the intellectual and moral world of man what the sun is to the planets in our system—the fountain and source of light and life, spiritual and eternal...The Bible, or the Old and New Testaments, in Hebrew and Greek, contains a full and perfect revelation of God and his will, adapted to man as he now is. It speaks of man as he was, and also as he will hereafter be: but it dwells on man as he is, and as he ought to be."

I couldn't deny how God and His Word had changed Masami's life. God began to use that transformation to work on me, even though I didn't want to admit it.

Salvation in the Land of Mormonism?

The state of Utah, the heart of Mormon country, seems like an unusual place for a person to become a Christian. But that's what happened to me.

A little over two years after arriving in the Azores, I was transferred to Hill AFB in Ogden, Utah. By the way, despite the military's warning that Masami would never be allowed in because "the computer says she's a communist," by God's grace, immigrating to the United States was no problem for her. I guess God knows how to deal with computers because she's now an American citizen!

To be honest, I was glad to move back to the States, away from the Azores. Utah was a whole new world for us, and growing up on the road I was ready for a change, quite frankly.

Surprisingly, even though I had seen the Lord change Masami's life, I still didn't want anything to do with the church. I believed I was already a Christian. I had the mistaken notion that the only time people really went to church was when they had problems. I didn't have any problems at the time, so I didn't feel the need to waste my time sitting in some building hearing about God.

After we arrived in Utah, we began to look for a place to live. The military told us that it would take three to five *years* for us to get a house on the military base, so we went off base looking for an apartment. The next day, we found one and signed a lease.

However, that same afternoon while I was at work, I got a call from a man who worked at the base housing office. He explained that an on-base house had just become available, and I was the first person he had been able to get in touch with. He had already called several people who were ahead of us on the waiting list, but hadn't been able to reach them. So we had the first shot at the home that had just come open.

We went to look at the house, and it was unbelievable! It had been the base commander's old home, and the backyard was actually the base's golf course. We had been authorized for only a three-bedroom house, but the military was offering us this large, beautiful, four-bedroom home. And the military even gave us a housing allowance to live in that home because they classified it as substandard since it was so close to the runway. It turned out to be the nicest house we had ever lived in and the airplane noise never even affected us. We were amazed by this opportunity. Of course, we accepted the offer immediately!

Since we had just signed an apartment lease that morning, I called the man in the apartment leasing office to let him know about the house. He graciously gave us back our deposit, even though he didn't have to. That was a real blessing to Masami and me, as finances were tight at the time.

I'll never forget what happened as we moved into our new home. Our neighbor was standing outside, so we walked over to greet her. As we introduced ourselves, she said, "You're Carl Kerby? I know you."

Surprised, I said, "No, I don't think we've met."

"Yes," she replied, "I'm sure I know you somehow."

She thought for a moment, and then suddenly it clicked. "Yep, that's it! I'm the secretary at the church down the street. Your pastor in the Azores wrote a letter telling us to be on the lookout for both of you, because you were moving here."

I couldn't believe it! I thought, *Come on. I came here to get away from all that church stuff!*

My wife, however, was so excited to know that there was a church waiting for us there. She told me, "I really want to go to church." I didn't.

Guess what else? In the entire state of Utah, only one Japanese church existed, and guess where it met? In the basement of the church where this woman worked as the secretary.

That Sunday, I took Masami to this lady's church. Masami attended the Japanese service, while I attended the English service. I didn't like the church at all. About two hundred and fifty people attended, and that was way too many for me. I decided that the next time I would stay home and Masami could just drive herself there.

Now, you have to understand that this was a major decision for us. Masami didn't have a driver's license while in Japan, where almost everyone gets around by bus, bike, or train. She had just learned how to drive while we were in the Azores, but there we had only one stoplight on the entire island! The only traffic hazards there were donkeys pulling carts on the quaint brick roads.

One day, after finishing a driving lesson in the Azores, Masami shared an interesting experience with me. As she was driving, the car's steering wheel had come right off of the steering column into her hands. The driving instructor simply stepped on the brake and told her, "Oops! Lessons are done for today!" Good call!

Now you know why I wasn't too excited about letting her drive in the U.S. I was concerned that she really didn't have enough experience on the road. In this case, though, the church was only about a mile and a half from our home, so I thought she could handle that drive. However, after the first Sunday we attended, the Japanese church disbanded and moved to downtown Salt Lake City—about thirty-five miles away! In order to get there, Masami would have to drive down a major interstate with a high speed limit and then into the city. She really wanted to attend the Japanese church. So every week, she was on my case about wanting to go to church, but I could not let her drive on the interstate and in a busy city with her limited driving experience.

I sat in the church pews every Sunday, listening to the pastor preach, but I didn't understand the gospel. I even talked the talk, yet I was lost as a goose.

Finally, I relented and started taking Masami and our children into Salt Lake City to the Japanese church. I discovered that only about fifteen to twenty people attended that church. My complaint had been that the other church was too large, so I couldn't say that this church was "too small." I was out of excuses so we began attending there regularly.

Around the same time, my brother Tony, who is eight years younger than me, began having some personal difficulties. He had started getting into trouble with the same things I had been involved in back in high school—in particular, drugs and alcohol. My parents grew worried and contacted me, and I offered to have my brother come out and live with us in Utah.

Masami and I still lived in that beautiful four-bedroom house on the golf course. By that time we had two young children, but we still had an extra bedroom sitting there vacant. The Lord had provided for us long before we even realized our need for this extra room! Remember, the Air Force had authorized us to receive only a three-bedroom home, but God knew what we would need in order to help my brother.

However, we did set one condition that my brother had to meet in order to be able to move in with us: he had to attend church with us. I thought, *Hey, if I have to go to church, he has to go to church!* I still was not a Christian at that point, but I had been taking my wife to church, and then I began taking my brother to church. You know, one of my greatest fears to this day is the knowledge that countless people attending church are just like I was back then. I sat in the church pews every Sunday, listening to the pastor preach, but I didn't understand the gospel. I even talked the talk, yet I was lost as a goose.

THE PIECES START COMING TOGETHER

The year 1987 was when God began to assemble many seemingly unrelated pieces of my life story and experiences. I've already shared with you how I was given a chance to go into the military and not have to face criminal charges for being drunk and disorderly. (I'm sure I would have been convicted, because I was guilty.) Truth be told, I've been caught by the authorities five times with marijuana and never been prosecuted. I still sometimes marvel at this, and find it hard to comprehend why God protected me so much.

In addition, I failed one of my tests in air-traffic control school because I was so hung over. I'll never forget the day my instructor called me into a room and asked, "What are you doing?" (Man, I wish I had a nickel for every time someone has asked me that question!)

"Based on your test scores," he continued, "you should be breezing through this school. Tomorrow I'm giving you a retest—and the next test, too. If you fail either one, I will not only kick you out of ATC, I'll have you kicked out of the Air Force!"

His words scared me to death because I had absolutely nothing to go back to. Needless to say, I never failed another test!

With few other options, my plan was to stay in the Air Force for twenty years and then retire. But God had different plans for me. My move to the Federal Aviation Administration (FAA) was very unexpected, and the way that it happened was unheard of at the time.

You see, typically when people want to enter the FAA, they have to pass a test and complete a special training program in Oklahoma before they can earn the federal job.

I had been in the military a little over eight years in 1987 when the Air Force forced me to make a decision. For whatever reason, they decided to require the military members who were within a year of discharge to either reenlist early or be discharged early from the Air Force. Since my plan was to remain in the military until retirement, I filled out the paperwork telling the Air Force that my plan was to reenlist.

Shortly before I submitted my final paperwork, I called a controller buddy of mine in Alaska (a man whom I had taught to be a controller in the Azores). During our conversation, he told me something that changed everything for me. "Carl," he announced, "I'm going into the FAA!"

"When do you leave for school?" I asked him incredulously. He informed me that he didn't need to go to school, because he was being hired as part of a special program. (The FAA was still looking to fill spots after a 1981 strike when many striking controllers were fired.) Evidently, the FAA had sent information packages to military bases around the U.S. to recruit controllers. I learned later that I hadn't heard of this recruiting effort because my chief controller had thrown away the package and the application forms. He didn't want his military controllers leaving!

Since the Air Force wouldn't let me go back overseas, which is where I wanted to be, I figured I would leave the military and go make more money in the civilian world. The only problem: my friend in Alaska told me that if I wanted to apply, my application had to be postmarked that day or the FAA wouldn't consider it. So I stayed up after my shift and hastily wrote a résumé (it was handwritten, in fact) and submitted some paperwork. It all looked terrible and unprofessional, but I had no time to do it correctly. I was able to get my application packet in the mail that day.

It was a few months before the FAA informed me, "You've got a job." I was ecstatic at first, until I learned that the FAA wanted to put me in what's called a "Center." Air-traffic controllers can work in three different places: Approach Control, where I was used to working; the Tower; or the Center. I had no experience working in the Center environment and very little Tower experience.

I told the FAA recruiter that while I had military experience in controlling, he was trying to place me in an area where I had no experience at all. I confessed that I probably wouldn't be able to do a very good job. However, the FAA was adamant: they needed people in the Center. "Well, I understand your situation and appreciate the offer," I told him, "but I'm just going to stay in the Air Force. But if you put me in Approach Control, I'll take the job."

So I continued with the reenlistment process in the Air Force.

A short time later I came home from work on a Friday and found a letter from the FAA in my mailbox. I was scheduled to sign my final Air Force reenlistment paperwork that following Monday. The letter informed me that the FAA was giving me a job, and that I was to be placed in Salt Lake City Approach Control! So I walked into my squadron commander's office on Monday and told him that I would not be reenlisting after all, but instead would be taking a job with the FAA. How was that for timing? God is rarely early, but He's never late, either!

I still was not a Christian at the time, but today I see how the Lord's hand orchestrated all of those events. I know He opened the door for me to get that job with the FAA. He was moving me toward something great and I was about to find out what it was.

THE SCALES ARE PEELED FROM MY EYES

My life changed forever on May 15, 1987, when evangelist Lowell Lundstrom came to Salt Lake City for a crusade. I believe this was the first time in the city's history that a major Christian evangelism outreach like this was held. The crusade was hosted at the Jon Huntsman Center at the University of Utah.

I urged my brother, Tony, to attend that evening because Mark Eaton, a basketball player for the Utah Jazz NBA team, was speaking. Both of us loved basketball, so I told my brother, "You've got to go hear this guy!"

That night, Rev. Lundstrom preached a simple, crystal-clear gospel message. For the first time, I understood that I was a sinner and that I would go to hell regardless of how "nice" I was unless I fell on my face before God and confessed my sin to Him. As I sat in the auditorium and watched hundreds of people walking forward to profess that they were surrendering their lives to Christ, the proverbial "scales" fell off of

Meeting with evangelist Lowell Lundstrom in December 2007

my eyes. At that moment, I just knew that I did not have a personal relationship with Christ and that I needed one.

Finally, everything "clicked" for me, and I recognized and admitted that I needed God in my life. I'm amazed now when I look back and see how the Lord prepared the way for my salvation experience.

Twenty years later, I had the privilege of meeting Pastor Lundstrom in December 2007. I had contacted him to see if I could meet him and thank him for his willingness to come to Salt Lake City and minister back in 1987 when I received Christ. What a blessing that meeting was!

Once I became a Christian, though, I had a big problem to overcome. Growing up with my kind of background, I didn't respect the Bible. To me, the Bible was just a "good book" full of stories that dealt with spiritual and moral issues. I didn't recognize its historical value or understand its authority as the Word of God. But my wrong thinking was about to change.

From the Cockpit to a Creation Ministry

One day I flew out to see my father in Oregon. As an air-traffic controller at the time, I could ride along in the airplane cockpit for training. Once we were in flight, I started to share my newfound faith in Jesus with the two pilots. It "just so happened" that both of them were Christians. What are the chances of that?

I truly enjoyed talking with these pilots about salvation and spiritual issues as we cruised along. But then somehow we got onto the topic of creation and evolution. I simply told the pilots what my first Sunday school teacher had taught me: that you can take the principles of evolution and just fit them in with what the Bible says. He had told me that there was no contradiction between Scripture and evolution, and I believed him. This was all I had ever heard and I had no idea there was even another way of understanding the Scriptures.

The copilot twitched a little as he straightened up in his seat, then glanced at the pilot before looking at me. "Carl," he said, "I'm sorry, but that's incorrect." He was blunt but loving at the same time.

"Why's that?" I asked.

Right there in the cockpit, he pulled out a Bible and started explaining creation to me. He read numerous Scripture passages and offered me many clear and logical facts that refuted both Darwinian evolution (that all life evolved purely by random processes from less complex life forms) and theistic evolution (the belief that God used evolution as part of creation and human history). I am eternally grateful to this man for his courage and faith. I now share this experience with my seminar audiences, and I always tell them, "*He started with the Word to explain the world.*"

> *Right there in the cockpit, he pulled out a Bible and started explaining creation to me. He started with the Word to explain the world.*

No one had ever done that for me before. In the past, sometimes Christians would offer their opinions (which may or may not be correct) and then they would go to the Bible to find verses that seemed to support their opinion. This is called "prooftexting." I later learned that all too often people "pull" verses out of the Bible without considering the context of the passage from which the verse is taken. (You can't make a verse say something that it didn't mean in the original context. That's called Scripture twisting.). This pilot started with the Bible and used it properly to explain to me a biblical position on creation.

DISCOVERING THE TRUTH IN *THE LIE*

After that copilot shared the truth about creation with me, I stared at him with astonishment and awe. "Where did you learn to think like that?" I asked him.

"From a book called *The Lie: Evolution* by Ken Ham," he told me. I had never heard of the book, the author, or the ministry he was associated with. (At the time Ken was with the Institute for Creation Research [ICR], formerly located in California, but now in Dallas, Texas.) I had never even heard of anything called a creation ministry. But I was intrigued, and just knew I had to read that book.

As soon as I returned to Salt Lake City, I called ICR and ordered *The Lie*. When it arrived, I eagerly read the whole book in one night. This was the first time I had ever grasped the correct

The Lie: Evolution by Ken Ham

way to approach creation and the Word of God. This book clearly showed me that the Bible wasn't just a "good book" containing some interesting stories and positive moral teachings. The Bible is a real history book, and one of the most accurate ever written. I learned that the Bible also deals with how we should live and how we should look at the world. It was a thrill for me to discover all these amazing truths.

After I finished reading *The Lie*, I called ICR and learned that they were planning to hold a "Back to Genesis" seminar in Salt Lake City. The person I spoke with gave me the name of one of the men in the area who was helping to lead the local steering committee. Several committed Christians were needed to organize these large regional seminars. I called him and offered to help. He told me that they were going to have another planning meeting soon, and that he would call me with the details.

I waited about two weeks and didn't hear anything, so I called the man again. He sheepishly told me, "We've already had the meeting." As I talked with him further, I realized that this group, having been somewhat successful in hosting a previous creation conference, had lost some of their excitement for hosting the next one. They had done the conference once before, and they seemed to have the attitude, "We already know what we're doing, so everything's on auto-pilot."

Another week or so went by and I still hadn't heard anything from the committee. So I called the man and reminded him that I wanted to be involved. He told me they were having another meeting the next night and invited me to attend.

I did, and the committee appointed me as the person in charge of facility preparation for the seminar. The event was set to take place on May 15, 1989. Interestingly enough, it was to be held at the Huntsman Center in Salt Lake City, where I had received Christ exactly two years earlier!

A few months before the seminar, Ken Ham, the author of the book *The Lie* that had been such a great help to me, flew out to Salt Lake City to host a pastors' breakfast. The breakfast meeting was designed to inform area churches of the upcoming seminar, and the pastors in attendance were asked to help promote it.

During this special pastors' meeting, Tim Rizor of ICR (who had flown out to assist with the meeting) learned that his father had just passed away. Tim and his wife, Joy, had to return to California immediately.

"I'm an air-traffic controller," I told Tim. "Let me make a few calls." I helped him in making preparations to fly back home to be with his grieving family. I was happy to be useful during this difficult time in Tim's life.

As he prepared to leave for the airport, Tim talked with Ken about the problem they now faced. The two were supposed to travel to Grand Junction, Colorado, later that day to set up for a two-day conference. Now, the question was, who was going to accompany Ken to Colorado to help set up all the equipment, train the volunteers, and oversee the dozens of tasks required for that conference?

Again, it was clear to me that this was one of those "sovereignty of God" moments—those moments that were so very exciting to a "baby Christian" like me. It just so happened that I had taken the entire week off from work as vacation time, but I wasn't planning to go anywhere. So I looked over at this team of leaders and said, "Hey, if you'd like, I'll volunteer to go to Grand Junction and help."

They accepted my offer, so I took a four-hour car trip with some of the other Salt Lake City committee members to help set up and run the seminar. It was really thrilling to see so many people turn out at the convention center in western Colorado, but most of all, I gained some tremendous experience that I was able to apply at our Salt Lake City conference that we would be hosting in just a few months.

A HEART-TO-HEART TALK WITH KEN HAM

At the Colorado seminar, I had many things I wanted to share with Ken. One evening as I was sitting next to him I told him, "You know, Ken, one of the ways this ministry has really affected me has been through the reading of your book *The Lie.*"

I shared with him that his book helped me to notice something sad about the church. I recalled that when I was a kid and would often ask questions, many times adults would pawn me off on a pastor or a teacher to get the answer, or they would tell me, "Shh! Good boys don't ask those questions!" or "Children are to be seen and not heard!" These experiences communicated something critical (but tragic) to me: that what I was asking about was really not that important to them and that they didn't have suitable answers.

When I went to the "world" (secular sources) and asked questions, my teachers would give me answers, whereas I didn't necessarily get them from the church. This revealed to me that, many times, those in the church were not equipped to share the truths of the Bible.

You see, my own children, who were in first and second grade at this time, had also begun coming to me asking spiritual questions. Almost all the students in their school were Mormons and were sharing with them what they were learning in the Mormon church. I realized that I had been doing the same thing that had been done to me: I was pawning my children off on somebody else because I didn't have the answers. And now they were getting answers from Mormons. After I read *The Lie*, it hit me: *as a Christian, I have to know the answers. I am responsible.* The book challenged me as a parent to realize that if I didn't provide answers (or attempt to find them) for my son and daughter, I was communicating a powerful (but wrong) message to them: that their questions really didn't matter and the Bible had a very limited application.

> *I realized I was pawning my children off on somebody else because I didn't have the answers. It hit me: as a Christian, I have to know the answers. I am responsible.*

I had recently read a newspaper article about the ten most intelligent people in America. Back then, the American public considered the scientist and evolutionist Dr. Carl Sagan to be the most intelligent person in the U.S. Why? According to those polled, "He seemed to have an answer for everything."

What struck me is that none of the top ten people on that list, to my knowledge, was born again. It seemed to me that if we

My "roadie" days, with Joy, Tim, Pastor Jim, and Ken

serve the all-knowing, all-powerful, and all-wise God who has given us His Word as our basis for living, shouldn't Christians —of all people—be on that list? At the very least, shouldn't Christians have answers for life's major questions and solutions for life's biggest issues? If so, then we would be seen as being authoritative and having the answers to people's questions about faith and the world.

Ken seemed to sense my heartbeat for ministry and my powerful desire to be able to present answers from the Bible. He encouraged me to get more involved with creation ministry. A day later, as I was about to leave that incredible Colorado seminar, he came outside to shake my hand and say good-bye. I couldn't even speak to him because I was trying to hold back tears.

I had been so moved as I watched what happened at that seminar in Grand Junction, Colorado. I had carefully watched the audience's reaction to Ken's talk, and it was so obvious that the "light bulbs" were going on in their heads. These people, for the first time, were grasping how important the Bible was in their lives, and that they didn't just have to take God's Word as merely a book of faith. They were discovering that Scripture is the sourcebook of all matters of practice, as well as faith. In fact, it is authoritative in all areas of life. The crowd's reaction deeply moved me (as it still does), and I knew that I had to get involved with creation ministry.

For approximately the next seven years, I traveled the country as a volunteer at many "Back to Genesis" conferences with ICR and then later with Answers in Genesis when Ken Ham started his own ministry. I attended as many conferences as possible, usually one or two a month. Initially with ICR I was responsible for setting up the book tables and the video equipment with Tim and Joy. I was a creation "roadie" of the highest degree, and I absolutely loved being a part of these life-changing conferences. I was hooked on creation ministry!

Remember the "Bottom Strip"!

I n the mid-1990s, I was still working as a civilian in air-traffic
control at the Salt Lake City Airport. As I mentioned, in
the air-traffic career field you can work in three different
areas: the Control Tower, En-route Center, or TRACON (Ter-
minal Radar Approach Control). My goal was to transfer to
Chicago's O'Hare TRACON to see if I could work at the world's
busiest airport. At that time if you wanted to talk to airplanes,
O'Hare was the place to be, and I truly wanted to know if I
could rise to the challenge. In addition, I was on the board of
directors for Answers in Genesis, and since it was closer to
their offices in the Cincinnati area it would allow me to do
even more volunteer work for the ministry. This was before I'd
even given my first talk!

Transferring to Chicago O'Hare required that I pass a rigorous test. In fact, the test took five days to complete! I had to
send in my résumé, and if they liked it, they would invite me
out to participate in the testing process. The requirements
were pretty challenging. Even before I got the job, I had to

memorize many details about every airport, including runway length, width, approaches, identifiers, and more.

The testing was done using a realistic computer simulation. Everything looked just like it did in the real world, complete with the same radar equipment that I would be using in approach control. The only difference was that in this simulated environment, a computer operator moved the airplanes across the scope by following my instructions. This was a very high-tech system, and it was light-years different from that in any other facility where I'd worked.

By God's grace, I became the first person in three months to pass the test. I give God all the credit. As I said before, I know where I should have been—in jail somewhere, serving time for all the things I had done before God saved me, or dead.

These kinds of open doors and remarkable experiences keep me mindful of God's blessings and compel me to thank Him for all that's happened. I can't take any of the credit. The prophet Jeremiah wrote that if you've got anything to "glory" about, glory in the Lord:

"But let him who glories glory in this,
That he understands and knows Me,
that I am the LORD..." (Jeremiah 9:24)

That's all I've got to glory about. It was God who brought me into that challenging exam at O'Hare and gave me the ability to pass the test. And even though I accepted the position, I knew that I would not be able to do that tough job on my own without God's help.

To learn the job of an Air-Traffic Controller (ATC), new employees need to be thoroughly trained by an experienced mentor/trainer. I soon met the person who was slated to teach me the job at O'Hare. I'll never forget what he told me one day. "Carl," he said, "everything you know about air-traffic

The training room at Chicago O'Hare Airport

control? Forget about it." With his heavy Chicago accent, he was somewhat intimidating. I felt like I had just walked into a Mafia movie and could almost envision this guy hitting me over the head with a pipe.

"What do you mean?" I asked.

"If you don't forget about it, you won't make it here at O'Hare!" he said bluntly.

Frankly, his words didn't make any sense to me. After all, hadn't I been hired because I had sixteen years' experience in air-traffic control? Hadn't I passed their rigorous test based on my prior knowledge and experience? I wondered, *What did they think got me to this point?*

While I worked at the Salt Lake City Airport (as well as in the Azores and Japan), I controlled five, six, maybe seven planes at a time. I might have had that many planes for twenty or thirty minutes, but then things would slow down. At Chicago O'Hare, when I got busy I typically had ten to twelve aircraft to manage, and for an hour or longer. As soon as I got rid of one aircraft, *boom*—it was immediately replaced with another. The atmosphere was pretty intense.

My "Mafia" mentor had been right: I had to get rid of my old way of thinking and completely relearn the job in a much more challenging environment. This reminded me of how a Christian, especially a new one, has to renew his thinking when he makes the transition from darkness to light and new life in Christ (Ephesians 4:22,23; Romans 12:2).

While working at O'Hare, I learned about three potentially deadly problems that can occur when a controller gets extremely busy. The first problem is "tunnel vision." That means the person gets so overwhelmed that he just focuses on one area under his responsibility. When that happened to me, all I could see was one small area with a couple of airplanes. The problem was that I was also responsible for ten other aircraft that were moving hundreds of miles an hour. If I hadn't learned to overcome tunnel vision and control all those planes, bad things could have happened, and fast!

Second, when a controller is overwhelmed, he often begins to speak very quickly. Sometimes I found myself talking faster and faster and faster. (To this day, my seminar audiences often tell me that I speak very fast. You should have heard me when I had ten pilots to instruct!) When I had that many airplanes, my adrenaline surged, and I tried to give as much information as I could as quickly as possible. However, this often backfired because when a controller speaks too quickly, the pilots may not understand a word he has said, or they may misunderstand and think he said something else. And that's dangerous.

"LOSING THE PICTURE"

By far, the worst thing that an ATC can do is called "losing the picture." This is when the person completely freezes. When this happens, he has so much going on that he doesn't even

Chapter 9

know where to start, and his mind just goes totally blank. Trust me, this isn't good!

In my over twenty-four years of working as an ATC, I "lost the picture" only one time. That was a very humbling experience, and one I wish I could forget. I was still in training, working departures from O'Hare headed westbound. The airport grew extremely busy. I had at least fourteen aircraft to manage at one time, and they just kept coming. I scanned the screen, and all of a sudden my mind went completely blank.

Imagine this: you're a violinist in a symphony and your solo is just about to begin. As the spotlight turns on you, you look down at the music, only to discover that the sheet in front of you contains nothing but meaningless dots and squiggles! So you freeze, unable to play a note.

That's what happened to me when I "lost the picture." All I saw were strips of paper and screens with flashing letters and dots moving in all directions with no meaning. I froze! I almost felt like I had entered the Twilight Zone. You would have thought that it was my first day in Air-Traffic Control School. I had no clue what to do!

Feel safe? Ready to fly in and out of O'Hare now? Don't worry; flying is very safe! Remember this: when a controller is learning the job, he is not by himself. He has a person sitting next to him, teaching him how to do the job. That trainer watches his every move and immediately corrects him when he has made a mistake.

The day that I "lost the picture," I immediately turned to the man who was teaching me and said, "Dude, you got it? I'm toast!" He had to jump in and take over, which (thankfully) he did very well.

As a controller, when things start to fall apart for you, your nearby colleagues can tell. Just by looking at the speeds of the aircraft, they know when a controller is on the verge of losing control. When this happens, you'll hear a reminder reverberating throughout the TRACON: "Bottom strip!"

What your colleagues are telling you is this: if everything is falling apart and you're losing control, the only way to get back in control is to find a basic point from which to start. Let me explain. As a controller, you have strips of paper in front of you, and each one represents an individual aircraft with its flight number, where the plane is coming from, and where it's going.

Below is a sample:

AWE 2	3163	ORD /	+IOW+		32L
					270
L/B752/E	P1525		ORD JOT J60 IOW./.PHX		
151	350				

Here's a basic breakdown of the information on this strip:

AWE: America West (also known as Cactus Airlines)

L/B752/E: The type of aircraft and the kind of equipment the aircraft has on board

ORD JOT J60 IOW./.PHX: This aircraft is leaving ORD (O'Hare) going to PHX (Phoenix). The information in between indicates the route the plane will take to get there.

Simple, right? Every time you get a new aircraft to control, you get a strip of paper that corresponds with it. You then place the newest strip above the strip for the previous aircraft that you received control of. The strip that's at the bottom gives you information for the airplane that you've controlled the longest. Depending on whether that plane is departing or arriving, it is either the closest or the farthest aircraft from the airport.

If that aircraft is arriving, you have the least amount of time to deal with it. For example, if the plane is arriving and is seven miles away from the airport, you have only about ninety seconds before you have to transfer the communication of that aircraft from you to the control tower. For the planes listed on the top strips, those flights might be fifty miles from the airport. In the world of air-traffic control, you've got a lifetime to deal with those planes; they're at least seven or eight minutes away. (In my world, that was a lifetime!)

This being the case, if you get locked in on any one area (tunnel vision) for any amount of time and fail to keep the big picture in focus, you can get into trouble very quickly.

Here's where the "bottom strip" comes into play. Remember, you need a starting point to focus on to help you regain control when everything falls apart. You start with the aircraft at the bottom of your pile of strips, the closest one to the airport when you're working arrivals, and start giving control instructions for that flight. Then you go up the line to the next one, and you continue to work your way up the strips.

But you don't just keep working your way to the top of the stack. After about the third or fourth plane, you have to go back to the bottom strip and start the process over. This time, though, your motives are different. You're no longer giving control instructions; you are checking to be sure that the pilot is actually following your instructions. Most of the time you don't say a word. You are just observing the position, heading, and altitude of the aircraft on the radar screen to make sure everything is okay and that the aircraft is doing what it was instructed to do.

We do this because there is a major problem that can happen in air traffic, as well as in life: sometimes we miscommunicate. For example, sometimes I would tell aircraft to do one thing, but the pilot would hear something else. For instance, I might tell an aircraft, "Delta 231, turn left heading three-six-zero."

The pilot would respond, "Roger, Delta 231 turn left heading two-six-zero."

When you read this, you can immediately see the problem. But when these instructions are spoken over the radio, this simple miscommunication is not as apparent. Over the radio, three-six-zero can sound very much like two-six-zero, and following these different sets of instructions would produce two completely different outcomes.

By the way, whose fault is it if that aircraft turns to a different heading than the one that I, as the controller, issued to him? If he responded back to me with the wrong information and I didn't catch it, it's *my* fault. To have effective and accurate communication, I not only have to give instructions correctly, I also have to ensure that the receiver understands and complies with my instructions.

So, whenever you "lose the picture" as an ATC, you simply go to the bottom strip and work your way through the strips for the planes that you've given instructions to, ensuring they are complying with your commands. Then, when you get to the place where you left off the last time, you start issuing instructions again to three or four aircraft. Immediately after giving those instructions, you go back to the bottom strip and work your way through the process again. You end up turning yourself into a human conveyor belt!

You spend almost twice as much time working through the strips, ensuring that everything is going well, as you spend giving instructions. In the end, you get back in control and regain the big picture this way.

So what does the "bottom strip" have to do with the Christian life? A lot! Here's the lesson I've drawn from this illustration and how I relate it to our walk with the Lord. All of us have a breaking point. All of us face times when we feel that our lives are out of control or that God has completely disappeared from our lives. As soon as we start feeling overwhelmed, we have to remember: go to the "bottom strip"!

Spiritually speaking, the "bottom strip" is the basics of our faith. We know that God exists. We know that He loves us. We know that He cares about our pain. We know that He sent His Son, Jesus, into the world to die on the cross for our sins and rise again so we can have eternal life. We know that we have abundant life here on earth and eternal life in heaven. Our bottom strip is not necessarily what we feel; it is what we know from the Word of God. And when we start to "lose the picture" we must return to our "bottom strip"—the foundation of our faith found in God's Word.

TOES TO NOSE AND LOOK FOR THE BOAT

Here is another excellent example from the book *The Art of Possibility* by the gifted husband-wife team of Rosamund and Benjamin Zander. (She is a psychologist and he is the conductor of the Boston Philharmonic Orchestra.) Rosamund writes:

> A dozen summers ago, I signed up for my first whitewater rafting trip, on Maine's Kennebec River. Traveling overland in a rickety bus to reach the launch point, I paid close attention to the guide standing in the aisle, as she undertook our education about this popular sport.
>
> "If you fall out of the boat," she said, "it is very important that you pull your feet up so that you don't get a foot caught in the rocks below. Think *toes to nose*," she stressed, and gave us a precarious demonstration, bracing herself and hoisting one foot toward her nose, "*then look for the boat and reach for the oar or the rope.*"
>
> Our guide chattered on as we bumped our way toward the river. Most of us had been on the road since

4 a.m. and were feeling sleepy and mesmerized by the vibrations of the bus. "Toes to nose," I heard again. And then, "look for the boat."

I thought, "Okay. That's fine, but I'm not going to fall out of the raft." Nevertheless, for the entire ride, she kept repeating the same instructions over and over. By the time we arrived at the river, I had heard it so many times, I felt slightly crazed, but just before we got into the raft, the guide asked again, "If you fall out of the boat, what do you say to yourself?"

"Toes to nose and look for the boat," we chimed back like a group of obedient gradeschoolers. A little while later, we surged into a stretch of Class 5 rapids. Suddenly, I was pitched into the water. I was roiling about underwater, completely disoriented. There was no up or down, neither water nor air nor land. There had never been a boat. There was no anywhere; there was nothing at all.

And then I heard the words, "Toes to nose..." emerging from a void. I pulled together into a ball. And then I heard from inside my head, "Look for the boat..." The boat appeared and then an oar. "Reach for the oar..." And I then found myself delivered back inside the boat, back into the world, traveling down the river.

I frequently tell the story of the raft trip in therapy and use the metaphor "out of the boat" to signify not only being off track in life but also not knowing where the track is anymore. When you are out of the boat, you cannot think your way back in; you have no point of reference. You must call on something that has been established in advance.[12]

I love this story. It drives home the same point as the story of the "bottom strip": when you get off course, you have to find a reference point in order to get back on track and out of danger. "You must call on something that has been established in advance." In life, the Bible is that reference point. Like the memorial stones, it reminds us of the faithfulness of our God and who we are in Him. I also find this story to be such a powerful example of why Scripture memorization is so important. We must hide the Word of God in our hearts and allow it to be imprinted on our minds. That way, when we are in a troubling situation, the Holy Spirit will bring those words to our remembrance (John 14:26), and they will guide us to make the right decision in those tough circumstances.

In Ephesians 4:14, Paul warns us about being tossed back and forth by every wind of doctrine. So to maintain a firm foundation, keep the Bible as your "bottom strip." Do you want to know how to deal with the issue of homosexual behavior? What about the abortion controversy? And how do we tackle the issue of creation and evolution? Here's the answer: the "bottom strip"—the foundational Word of God.

As I mentioned earlier, in order for me to learn ATC at O'Hare, I needed someone who was already trained and qualified to sit next to me, train me, and mentor me. It took a little over a year for me to be able to learn how to handle that level of traffic. It wasn't automatic; I had to be disciplined and focused on learning the job.

I believe we need this type of training and mentoring program in the church today. We need seasoned, knowledgeable Christians to sit down and show the next generation of Christians how to deal with a culture that is openly antagonistic toward our faith.

When you start with the Word of God and truly trust it as real history (not just a storybook full of fables and good moral values), you will be able to deal with the questions and the pressing issues that you face each day. As a result, you will come to conclusions that are different from what the secular world will tell you.

Unfortunately, many Christians these days don't know their Bible very well at all. And have you noticed that a lot of churches don't go very deep into the Word anymore? As a result, many Christians are more likely to think like people out in the world. They try to take man's "wisdom" and squeeze it into the Word of God (for example, trying to force theistic evolution to fit into the creation accounts in the book of Genesis). But if you start with the Word of God, you can find solid, satisfying answers—and they will almost always be different from what the world teaches.

Sadly, many Christians are scared to share their faith. They're afraid to broach issues like the creation/evolution debate because they don't want to be seen as weird. They don't want to risk being labeled "judgmental," "narrow-minded," or a "fundamentalist." But we need to remember that people are just people. They really don't have any power over us. They need the hope that comes through a saving relationship with Jesus Christ.

Don't be afraid to say, "Yes, I'm a Christian. I love God, and I love people. I believe in the Word of God. And that's going to be my stand. The Bible is my absolute authority in life."

One of my favorite verses is James 1:8, which warns us of the dangers of being "a double-minded man, unstable in all his ways." A double-minded person—one who has one foot in the Word and the other in the world—is on shaky ground and will be unstable in all that he does. However, when we start from God's Word as our foundation, we can be focused, single-minded believers. We can grow to become solid, stable Christians who are "rightly dividing the word of truth" (2 Timothy 2:15).

CHAPTER 10

Arrested Development: How My Speaking Ministry Began

People often ask me how I got involved with creation ministry. As I mentioned, years ago, I began speaking worldwide on the topics of Genesis, creation, and biblical authority; however, it took quite a circuitous route for me to get to where I am today. I always tell people, "If you want to become a speaker, don't take the route I did!"

You see, I never planned to be a speaker. My dad was a professional wrestler, for goodness sake. It's not like my background qualified me to engage in a creation vs. evolution ministry! I was the guy doing the behind-the-scenes work, setting up and tearing down. I've always been good at physical labor, so I was comfortable doing that. But God had other plans.

As I mentioned, I didn't graduate from high school because I hadn't passed senior English. It wasn't until I was in the Air Force that I took an English class to complete that requirement and received a high school diploma. Over the years, I've taken a lot of college courses, but all I had was an associate's degree until January 2011, when I finally graduated from Tennessee Temple University with a Certificate of Biblical Studies.

I was in college for over thirty years before graduating—how sad is that?

When I began volunteering for the Institute for Creation Research and met all of its Ph.D.-wielding scientists, the thought never entered my mind that I could ever speak to audiences on creation. How did this miracle occur? It happened after I convinced Ken Ham to embark on a speaking tour in my beloved Japan. But it took Ken being arrested by the authorities in Japan for me to begin speaking! How's that for a hook to get you to read more? Here's what happened.

Ken agreed to travel to Japan on a speaking tour on one condition: that Masami and I would go with him. He wanted us to help him navigate the culture, especially since we knew the language. That was a no-brainer! I love Japan and its people, so I said, "Absolutely. We'll go!"

We left for Japan in July 1996 for about a ten-day tour. Ken was scheduled to fly to Japan from Australia, where he was on a speaking tour. Masami and I were set to fly in from the United States. We arrived in Japan a little earlier than Ken to take care of the details, and we planned to have everything set up by the time he landed, so we could just pick him up at the airport and head off.

When Ken's flight arrived, we watched with anticipation as the arriving passengers walked through the airport's concourse. People kept coming out of baggage claim, but we never saw Ken. Finally, the last person walked out of baggage claim and passed us, and that was it. No Ken.

We waited and waited. Still no Ken. After waiting for about thirty more minutes, I decided to walk toward the security area near customs and the baggage carousel. An alarm went off as I walked into the area. With today's heightened security at airports, I would probably be put in jail just for walking back there! Several security officers came running toward me and began asking me questions. As we talked, I recognized Ken's suitcases sitting off to the side of the baggage carousel.

I explained to the security staff that I had been waiting a long time for the person whose suitcases were off in the distance. I asked, "Where is the man whose suitcases are over there?"

"You're waiting for him?" they asked.

"Yes!" I said.

"Go outside," they told me. "We'll have him call you."

Hmm. That didn't sound good. Finally, Ken called me and said, "Carl, they're not going to let me into the country."

Ken explained the problem. He had been living in the United States as an "alien" on a green card. (Since then, Ken has become a U.S. citizen.) The Australian airline Qantas had helped him arrange his flights from the U.S. to Australia to Japan. The Qantas staff had informed him that because he was living in the U.S. on a green card, he didn't need a visa to enter Japan. (Ken's travel agent had told him the same thing.) So Ken flew to Japan via Australia, and guess what? He did need a visa!

So, the airport security in Japan kept Ken from entering the country. To keep him and his wife from having to go to the "real" immigration jail, they offered to let us pay to have him stay in a hotel room for the night with a guard outside his door. But that hotel room and guard cost $800, and we had to pay in cash. Ouch! We all had to empty our wallets to come up with the money.

The police allowed me only five minutes in the guarded hotel room to speak with Ken. As I entered the room, I immediately asked him, "What are we going to do now? You're supposed to start your speaking tour tomorrow."

Ken took out his overhead transparencies (this was long before laptops and PowerPoint) containing all of his teaching points and illustrations. "You're it!" he told me.

I must have looked stunned. But Ken tried to encourage me by saying, "You've been around long enough, Carl. You know the message. You can do it!" So that's how I was thrust rather unwillingly into speaking on Genesis and creation!

I'll be honest with you: the first time I spoke was a horrible experience, both for me and for my audience. My Japanese isn't good enough for me to speak on my own, so I spoke through a translator. However, I would be right in the middle of a sentence when my translator would start translating, cutting me off. Then he'd finish and look at me, and I'd stare back at him with a blank look on my face. Most of the time, by the time he had finished translating, I had completely "lost the picture," but this time without a "bottom strip"! I couldn't even remember the first part of the sentence that I had just spoken. As you can imagine, it was pretty sad. I feel sorry for everyone who had to listen to me talk that day!

Perhaps the only "good" thing that came out of this experience was the fact that my talk was videotaped. I think Masami still has this video at home somewhere, and if I ever get too full of myself, all she would have to do is mention that videotape to bring me down to earth!

As a matter of fact, the talk went so badly, I believe that our Japanese hosts activated the National Early Warning System and made emergency calls all over Japan to the venues where Ken was scheduled to speak. I think the hosts told the others, "You've got a *big* problem. The replacement is *terrible*. You have to get another speaker." They started planning to have creation speakers fly in from the hinterlands of Japan to fill in for me.

For the next two days, I felt terrible about how that first meeting had gone. "I don't ever want to speak again. This is not my thing," I told Masami. "I'm content to set up tables and video equipment and do all the behind-the-scenes stuff. I feel that's really what God has called me to do."

So for the next two events, all I did was stand up all mealy-mouthed and tell the audiences what had happened to Ken. I apologized that he couldn't be there, and then I sat down while a last-minute replacement speaker gave a talk.

A SECOND CHANCE

For the fourth event, we traveled to Yokaichi for a big pastors' conference. The organizers there had also scrambled to find a replacement speaker. At the same time, the head pastor, Rev. Horikoshi, wanted to give me twenty minutes to speak to the other pastors who were attending the conference.

I wasn't very excited about the prospect of speaking to so many Christian leaders. I even told this man that I was fine with just giving an extended apology about why Ken couldn't

Rev. Horikoshi with his wife, Hama, with Masami and me in 2011

be there. But Rev. Horikoshi said, "No, please take twenty minutes and share with the pastors." Very apprehensively, I agreed.

This time, however, my translator was an American named Nathan Elkins who had been raised in Japan. His Japanese is impeccable. His father, a missionary, told me that he had dedicated his son to ministering in Japan. This guy was an amazing young man. In fact, he already knew quite a bit about the arguments for creation vs. evolution because he had previously translated for Dr. Duane Gish of the Institute for Creation Research. Dr. Gish was a well-known creation speaker and famous debater. Nathan even knew many of the unusual terms that are specific to the creation/evolution issue.

I stood up in front of these pastors and spoke for twenty minutes, and this time, the pastors and other Christian leaders were engaged and visibly excited. Nathan was so easy to work with, and I could tell that his translation was extraordinary. The entire process was seamless—the complete opposite of what my first speaking engagement had been like. From the audience's response, I could tell that Nathan had done a fantastic job of translating the nuances of my arguments for creation science.

As a matter of fact, after I had finished speaking, the host pastor approached me. "Carl, I'm so sorry," he said. "I didn't realize that you were a speaker. If I had known that, I would have given you more time." I was shocked! But after that experience, I was also greatly encouraged. Despite my shortcomings, I could see that God was using me to connect His truth with the audience in a very real way.

For the fifth speaking event, Ken finally was able to reenter Japan. He had been forced to fly back to Australia to get the issues all sorted out. While Japanese officials initially had told him that there was no way he could get a visa quickly and that it would take a minimum of two weeks, someone in a high position at the Japanese embassy in Australia had been sympathetic to his predicament and made it possible for him to be back in Japan in five days. We were later told that someone from the embassy in Japan had actually come to the Japanese airport to allow Ken to enter the country, but he had missed Ken's outbound flight to Australia by about ten minutes.

An interesting side note to all this is that a short time after leaving Japan, I noticed on the news that Japan was no longer requiring visas for people visiting from Australia. I immediately called Ken, and we laughed about this policy change. A friend of ours, Dan Lietha, even created this cartoon as a joke:

WELCOME TO JAPAN, KEN HAM!

VISA . . . DON'T LEAVE HOME WITHOUT IT!

Yes, it was a difficult experience during that time, but I can now see that things happened according to God's perfect plan. I had become quite comfortable being a behind-the-scenes kind of guy, but the Lord used these events in Japan to, in essence, tell me: No, Carl. I want you to step up now and do something else. That first speaking event was the catalyst for me to begin speaking in front of large groups of people. I certainly didn't plan it that way, but God did. He took the very rough-edged piece of my first speaking attempt and had a perfect place for it to fit in the mosaic of my life.

WISE WORDS

When I first started my speaking ministry, I was a full-time air-traffic controller, and I would travel on the weekends doing ministry. Pastor Phil was my pastor, and he really taught me an important lesson. Every week after I returned from ministry, he would ask me the same question: "How'd it go, Carl?" I didn't know how to answer that question. Frankly, I struggled with it, so I'd joke it off. I don't know how many times I told him something like, "Oh, nobody threw anything, so I guess it went pretty well."

He kept asking me this question, so after about three months, I finally broke down and got real with him. I said, "Pastor, I don't know how to answer that question. To be honest, I've been in meetings where the person who is speaking isn't making any sense to me at all. I just keep looking at my watch, wondering if it's still working, because time's not progressing at all. But sure enough, at the end of the meeting, one of the audience members will walk up to the speaker, pat him on the back, and tell him how much his talk meant to that person. I just don't put a lot of stock into people patting me on the back or telling me, 'That was really good.'"

I continued, "Sometimes, I feel like something powerful was accomplished through my speaking, like the time I had a pastor stand up in front of his congregation and tell them that he had been double-minded and he was committing to his congregation to be single-minded and stand firm on the Word of God from then on. I've also seen fathers who have walked up to me after I finished speaking and told me that they have committed to being a better father and a better husband after the meetings. That's when I really feel like something was accomplished."

I love Pastor Phil. I realized that he had been waiting for three months for me to be straight with him. He had set me up to make his point. He looked me in the eyes and said, "Carl, you're wrong!"

Ouch! I was pretty surprised by his response. "Why's that?" I asked him.

"How long did Noah preach?" he replied.

I thought about it and said, "Hmm. It depends on who you ask, but at least fifty years?"

"And how many people responded to his preaching?"

"Only his family members —seven others besides himself."

"Carl, if you base your success in ministry on the response of others, you will always be lonely in ministry," he said. "You have to ask yourself, 'Was I obedient?' And if you were obedient, you were successful regardless of whether or not anybody responded."

It's not my job to convict or convert people; it's my job to converse with people. The Holy Spirit will do the work of convicting and converting.

He was right. His wise words have made ministry so freeing for me. They took all the burden off me. It's not my job to convict or convert people; it's my job to converse with people. The Holy Spirit will do the work of convicting and converting.

My job is simply to be obedient, open my mouth and give an answer for the reason for my hope. And I do my job with God's help, you'd better believe the Holy Spirit will do *His* job!

Another one of my greatest ministry mentors, who shared some words of wisdom with me, is a man named Don Chittick. I met Dr. Chittick in Canada on one of my first ministry trips. I was still working as a "roadie" at this time. After he had finished speaking, I had the opportunity to talk with him, and he told me how he got involved with ministry.

He had been a professor at George Fox University, a Christian university in Oregon, and resigned in order to go into full-time ministry. At the very beginning of his ministry, he was scheduled to speak at a high school in Beaverton, Oregon, but a huge ice storm hit the night before. Although the school was not far from his home, it took him and his wife a crazy amount of time to drive there, and they arrived to find just a handful of cars in the parking lot. Only a few people had braved the storm to hear his talk.

"Carl, when I spoke, I gave them everything I had," he shared with me. "But when I finished, I was so discouraged. We got in the car, drove a block, then pulled over, and I just cried! I felt like I must not have heard God correctly. He must not have wanted me to go into ministry after all."

He then told me how recently, many years after his initial visit to that school, he was called back there to speak again. This time the auditorium was packed. After he had finished speaking, a man walked up to him and asked, "Do you remember that night you were here so many years ago?"

Dr. Chittick laughed and said, "Yes, I remember that night very well!"

"Well, I'm the senior high school science teacher here," the man continued. "I never told you this, but I videotaped your talk that night. I have shown it to every one of my graduating classes since then. I hope you don't mind!"

Wow! Dr. Chittick's talk had much more of a widespread impact than he ever knew. Thousands of students had heard his talk and had been influenced by it. In fact, some of them may have been led to trust in Christ as a result of it.

Dr. Chittick's story made it very clear to me that I shouldn't worry about how many people are in the audience when I speak. That's God's job. He will bring who He wants to bring. My job is to be obedient and speak the truth to those He has brought.

These two godly men served as mentors for me, helping me to grow as a Christian and as a speaker. The words of wisdom that they shared with me can also be an encouragement for you. As we give a defense of our faith, we don't have to worry about converting people, just conversing with them. Our job is just to open our mouth and speak the truth to those God brings to us. He will do His job; now let's do ours!

Whether speaking to a small handful or a full house, it's always a blessing to help people learn to defend their faith!

Becoming a Godly Father and Husband

W hile I continued to travel and speak about the authority of the Bible, God was also teaching me many truths about the kind of godly husband and father that I need to be. I began to realize that rearing our children to know and love God is one of the most important tasks that any parent could ever have.

Masami and I have two children, both born in Tokyo, Japan, while I was stationed there in the Air Force. Our daughter, Alisa (married to Bob Alcock, a paramedic), works in the public schools teaching English as a Learned Language. Our son, Carl Jr. ("Dennis"), is married to Tish, who is from South Africa. Dennis works as the manager at a photography studio as well as, I'm thrilled to say, with me at Reasons for Hope.

I'll never forget an incident that happened right after I received Christ in 1987. As I was getting dressed to go to work, a photo on my dresser caught my eye. It had been sitting there for a while, but for some reason, it was like God tore the blinders off my eyes and I saw that picture for the first time.

It was a photo of me seated, with my four-year-old daughter on my lap, outside an amusement park. What a great picture, right? A loving dad taking his children to the amusement park and enjoying the day? Wrong! When I saw that picture, I recalled exactly what I was thinking when it was taken. I was thinking, *This kid is heavy! I wish she would get off me!* I even had my arm in the small of her back, trying to gently push her off my lap.

Man, I just broke down when I remembered that. Only a day or two earlier, I had read in Exodus 20:5, "God visits the iniquity of the fathers upon the children to the third and fourth generations of those who hate Me." I started crying because I realized I was treating my children the way I felt I had been treated as a child. Growing up, I'd always felt I was a bother.

With my dad as a wrestler, our family was moving all the time. I don't think I lived in any one place for more than a couple of years. I had to learn how to fit in and adapt to a variety of environments, so I became a pretty good "chameleon," constantly changing to fit whatever environment I was thrown into. I never really felt loved and accepted for who I was, because I didn't really know who I was. Since I never felt confident about myself, I didn't establish close relationships with anyone. I always thought if people "knew" me, they could hurt me, so I gave them just enough information so they couldn't.

The day that I "saw" that photo with spiritual eyes, I knelt down and confessed my sin, sincerely asking God to forgive me and change me. I didn't want to have a strained and distant relationship with my children or my wife. But letting go of this coping mechanism was very difficult. It took time.

Over the years, the Lord softened my heart and taught me how to be more authentic and transparent with others. The greatest compliment my daughter paid me was during her senior year in high school. She was very frustrated with me one day, and in exasperation, she said, "Dad, 24/7! You want to be around us 24/7!"

My reply was, "Yes, and your point is what?" I really did want to be around my children 24/7.

After our kids left for college, Masami and I went into full-time ministry with Answers in Genesis and moved from Chicago to their headquarters in Kentucky. I thought we would "lose" the children, assuming they would want to stay in the Chicago area where all of their friends were. But after they graduated from college, both of our kids blessed us by moving to Kentucky so they could live close to us. Alisa called me a few months before graduation and said, "Dad, when I graduate, I want to come home!" (I bawled that day as well.) Our children now live within twenty minutes of us. God has been very good to us!

INVESTING IN OUR CHILDREN

I discovered very early that I could not trust the public school system to instill Christian values in my children. One very alarming statistic I learned is that "88 percent of the children raised in evangelical homes leave church at the age of 18 never to return."[13] I hear complaints all the time about what the government or the public schools are doing (or not doing) that is causing children to rebel and get into all kinds of trouble. The biggest trouble of all is children walking away from God. And that problem does not start in the White House, or in the schoolhouse, or even in the church house. The problem starts in *our house*. If we're losing 50 to 88 percent of the children raised in our homes to the world, we have to quit blaming everybody else and do something about it.

To all of you men reading this: please remember that it's not the government's job, the school's job, or the church's job to raise and train your children to love and serve God. It's not even your wife's primary responsibility. The Bible says it's *your* job.

Both moms and dads (and extended family, including the church family) are to help "train up a child in the way he should go" so that "when he is old he will not depart from it" (Proverbs 22:6). But, fathers, we are given a very specific command: "And you, fathers, do not provoke your children to wrath, but bring them up in the training and admonition of the Lord" (Ephesians 6:4). When we abdicate the responsibility of training our children in the Lord's ways to other people or institutions, trust me: we will not like the outcome.

It all begins in the home. As Christian husbands, we must start living out the biblical example of loving our wives as Christ loves the church and being willing to die for them. We start with that sacrificial love and assume the responsibility of leading our families. Until we do that, we can never expect the next generation (the Mosaics and even younger) to believe that we truly believe the Bible.

A friend once told me, "Carl, our children are like a bank account." I didn't get it, so he explained:

> I hear so many parents complaining about losing their teenage children that were raised in the church. Well, if you open a bank account and put nothing in it for eighteen years, and then come back to take out a withdrawal, don't expect to get much out. If we don't invest in our children their entire lives, we'll never get much of a "withdrawal" from them. If you've poured into them, trained them, and loved them, when the teenage years come and the peers start to have influence on them, you'll still, Lord willing, be able to see fruit in their lives, because you've invested spiritually and physically in their lives!

Am I saying that your child will never go in a wrong direction if you do your best to love and train them? Absolutely not! Our children are unique, created beings who have to establish their own personal relationship with Jesus Christ. And there will be times when, in spite of the parents' best efforts, children will walk away from the church and/or family. We have to remember in those times that God is still in control.

After he had explained it this way, his words made perfect sense to me, and I've done my best to pour my life into loving my wife and children ever since that day.

One of the ways I was able to have spiritual influence on my son was by teaching his Royal Ambassadors class when he was a young boy. One week, the boys were assigned Psalm 119:105 to memorize. The following week, they were supposed to recite the verse for me. The first lanky young man came up, took a big breath, and then spat out, "Thy word is a lamp unto my feet and a light unto my path" as quickly as he could.

"Good job!" I told him.

The next young man walked up, took an even bigger breath and then said, "Thy word iza lamp unto my feet anda light unto my path" even more quickly.

The third young man was named Ricky. I loved Ricky, and I still pray for him. He came up, took a huge breath and then spat out, "Thywordizalampuntomyfeetandalightuntomypath"! Yes, he had set a new world record, saying the verse in about 2.2 seconds. He was so happy! But then I did the unthinkable. I said to him, "That's great, Ricky, but what does it mean?"

The blank look on his face is still impressed on my mind to this day. "What does it mean?" he said. "What do you *mean*, what does it mean? No one's ever asked us that before!"

"Well, it's great that you can spit it out in 2.2 seconds," I said. "But what good is that if you don't know what it means?"

Then I had an idea. I told them, "Okay, everybody, get on that side of the room."

They all looked at each other as if to say, "What in the world is going on?"

"Go on, get on that side of the room." This was all off-the-cuff!

"Now, your job is this. I want you to get from that side of the room to the other side of the room as quickly as you can without touching any of the tables or chairs. Can you do it?" They ran across the room.

"That was boring," they said. "That was so easy."

"Okay, now I'm going to blindfold you, and I'm going to move the tables and chairs around so that some of them are lying on their sides with the legs sticking out. Then I'm going to tie your hands behind your back, and I want all of you to run to the other side. Can you do it then?"

"No way, we don't want to do that!" they responded.

"Why?" I asked them.

"Because we'll get hurt. When we run, the tables and chairs will hit our legs, and that'll hurt."

"Guys, that's the truth of Psalm 119:105," I told them. "God's Word is like a spotlight that we can shine into the darkness to help us keep from getting hurt. Those chairs and tables represent sin. God has given us His Word so that we don't have to make the same mistakes as those who lived in the past. We can go through life and not get beat up. We've got to trust His Word, though, or it will never work."

This truth really seemed to impress them. In fact, my son still remembers that illustration of Psalm 119:105, even though he's now a grown man with a son of his own.

Another of my favorite Scripture passages that offers instruction to fathers and sons is Psalm 78:1–8:

Give ear, O my people, to my law;
Incline your ears to the words of my mouth.
I will open my mouth in a parable;
I will utter dark sayings of old,
Which we have heard and known,
And our fathers have told us.
We will not hide them from their children,
Telling to the generation to come the praises of the
LORD,
And His strength and His wonderful works that He
has done.

For He established a testimony in Jacob,
And appointed a law in Israel,
Which He commanded our fathers,
That they should make them known to their children;
That the generation to come might know them,
The children who would be born,
That they may arise and declare them to their children,
That they may set their hope in God,
And not forget the works of God,
But keep His commandments;
And may not be like their fathers,
A stubborn and rebellious generation,
A generation that did not set its heart aright,
And whose spirit was not faithful to God.

Again, as fathers, it's one of our primary responsibilities to instill biblical values in our children and teach them to love and serve God. Unfortunately, we often focus more on helping our sons and daughters excel at sports, academics, and other activities than we do on helping them live godly lives. Take a look at your weekly calendar. How many hours do you devote per week to intentionally teaching biblical truth to your children? How much time do you spend nurturing your kids' spiritual health and development? I'd bet most of us spend more time on secular and non-church activities.

Voddie Baucham, author of *Family Driven Faith: Doing What It Takes to Raise Sons and Daughters Who Walk with God*, writes, "If I teach my son to keep his eye on the ball but fail to teach him to keep his eyes on Christ, I have failed as a father."[14]

When my son was in high school, I coached his basketball team. I wanted to pour into these young men spiritually, so after the first year I decided to take them on a mission trip to Jamaica. I had been there the year before and had made some excellent friends in the ministry.

Fairview Baptist College runs a very good summer camp there, so we made plans to help them out. Our job was to run basketball clinics and work as counselors at the camp.

I decided to invite my best "spiritual" players rather than just those who were the most talented at basketball. We got five godly young men together and started preparing for the trip. In one of my talks to help prepare them, I told them we were going as servants. "If they ask us to sweep, we'll sweep. If they ask us to clean, we'll clean. We're going to serve!"

Of the five young men planning to go, only one (my son) had been out of the United States. Of the other four, only one had even been out of the state of Illinois. They were pretty much white, Christian-schooled young men with no familiarity with any other cultures, so needless to say they were in for quite an experience.

One area I was concerned about was the food. I knew the boys might be confronted with foods that they were not accustomed to eating. I've been on many trips like this in a variety of circumstances and I know that strange foods can be a real issue. So I shared with them a motto that I had heard: "Lord, where You lead I will follow, what You feed I will swallow!"

One day on our trip while we were eating lunch, it happened. One of the young men had found something in his soup and was holding it up with his spoon inspecting it. I saw him out of the corner of my eye and laughed.

After a few moments he called out, "Hey, Coach, what is this?" I told him, "It's a chicken's foot." We were eating chicken foot soup! I cannot forget the look on his face as he said, "*A chicken's foot!!!*" I still laugh as I think of it. It was so funny. I cautioned him, "Remember what I told you!"

Honestly, though, everybody did fantastic. It was an amazing summer and we all grew spiritually. And now, so many years later, at least three of the young men who accompanied me on that mission trip serve in full-time, vocational ministry. What an encouragement for me and a blessing for them. God is so good!

SHAPED BY MY FATHER

After I became a Christian, I had to learn what the Bible says about being a godly role model as a father and husband. Most of my thinking about being a father and husband was shaped by my early experiences growing up with my father, who did not know the Lord. I was thirteen years old when my parents divorced. I loved both of my parents, and even though our relationship wasn't what I would have liked, I know that they loved me, too. The time surrounding their divorce was extremely difficult for me. But I knew that I could not follow my father's example in marriage and fatherhood.

I've heard some people say that there is such a thing as a "good" divorce, but you won't find that in the Bible. God says clearly that He hates divorce; broken marriages are not His desire for people (Malachi 2:16; Mark 10:6–9). So while divorce is bad according to God's Word, I know from personal experience that He can redeem it. In my case, despite the pain of my parents' divorce, the Lord used it to guide me in a new direction to a place and time when I would ultimately meet My heavenly Father and establish a relationship with Him.

Back when I was thirteen, I remember coming home from school one day and finding that most of our possessions were missing from our trailer. My uncle had stolen almost everything because he knew my parents were getting divorced. My mother took me and my three younger siblings to an apartment. After my mother remarried, we lived with her and my stepfather.

A short while after my parents' divorce, I experienced the scariest moment of my life. My father came back to town after being on the wrestling circuit for a while. He had remarried by that time, and I vividly remember sneaking away to see him. (My mother wasn't too excited about me spending time with my father.) I remember sitting with him and his new wife when he said, "Carl, I want you to come and live with us." To this day, I can remember the fear and insecurity that I felt when he made this request.

You may be wondering, *Why would this question be so scary?* Well, I can tell you, it's not for the reasons you may be thinking. I wasn't afraid of Dad because of discipline. My father was 6'8" and weighed 350

Me at about age 9, with brother Tony, relaxing with Dad on his time off

Around age 7, helping Dad display his two championship belts

pounds, yet he was one of the nicest men you could ever meet. In fact, I can remember being spanked by him only a couple of times in my life, and during one of those times, he was weeping about having to do it. Despite his tough-guy wrestling image, he was just a big, gentle teddy bear at heart. So discipline wasn't the reason I was afraid.

In fact, if I had been afraid of discipline, I never would have stayed with my mother! She was the disciplinarian in our house. If I messed up, which I did quite often, Mama would "get my mind right," so to speak! But let me be fair; I was not an easy child to raise, especially after the divorce. I was hurt and upset about my parents' split, and as a result, I grew very rebellious.

If I had been looking for an easy way out, I would have gone with Dad. As a teenager, I wasn't looking for discipline; I was looking for fun. And my dad really was the fun one. The few times we traveled with him, I had a blast on the road as we went from town to town.

It wasn't for moral reasons, either, because I wasn't a Christian at that time. I didn't understand that my father's life was not good. He hid his alcohol, drug consumption, and adultery from me.

So while you might think it would be a "no-brainer" for me to go live with my dad as an immature thirteen-year-old boy, I was scared to death at the thought of leaving my mom. In my heart, I just knew it would be wrong for me to go live with my father. So I told him that I wanted to stay with my mother.

That decision changed my relationship with my father for the rest of his life. I saw him no more than a dozen times after that. We did also talk by phone, but there were times when he would disappear for a couple of years. He couldn't accept the fact that I had chosen to stay with my mother and later allowed my stepfather to adopt me when I turned sixteen. (My birth name is Carl Dennis Campbell, Jr. When I was adopted, I took the last name Kerby.)

I'm confident that this is another case of God protecting me even before I received His gift of salvation. The Holy Spirit was convicting me and guiding me, warning me of the consequences of making a bad decision. As I mentioned, I knew it would be wrong for me to go with my father, even though on the surface it sure would have been easier.

Please keep in mind—especially you young people—that your decisions, both major and minor, *always* have consequences. Don't ever sell out for what a person can give you, because whatever someone can give you, someone else can take away.

More than thirty years have passed since I decided to stay with my mother. That decision was heartbreaking because I really wanted to maintain a relationship with my father, too. I tried. But I was never able to have the close, authentic relationship with him that I desired.

On November 12, 1997, I got a phone call that changed many things for me. This was soon after the creation meetings in Japan. That day, when I got home, I pressed the button on my answering machine and heard this message: "Carl, this is Mom. Please give me a call, it's important." In my heart, I already knew what must have happened.

You see, the day before, I had found out that Dad was in the hospital. He had been there for over a week, but for some reason, no one had let me know. I immediately called and spoke with him. He'd had a heart attack, but he seemed to be feeling better and he was in good spirits, even though his voice sounded weak.

That conversation means so much to me. I told my dad that I was coaching my son's high school basketball team. I also told him that I was very involved with ministry and that the next day I had my first official talk as a representative of Answers in Genesis. I was slated to speak at an AWANA banquet on the subject of "Dinosaurs and the Bible."

Dad told me that after he was released, he wanted to come and visit me. He wanted to see me coach my son's basketball team, and he wanted to visit his grandchildren. We spoke for about forty minutes, and then I told him I loved him and we said good-bye. He told me, "I love you too, son!" I was so encouraged and excited. I fully believed that this was a turning point for us and that our father-son relationship could be fully restored. Little did I know that this would be the last time I would ever speak to my father.

The day after that conversation, I received my mother's message on my answering machine. I just knew: Dad had died. I called her back and, sure enough, he had passed away. I was devastated. I don't know how I did it, but I went and spoke that evening. I can't even remember giving the talk. All I remember is finishing, turning it over to the pastor to close, and getting off the stage quickly. I ran to the back of the church auditorium and broke down crying.

I attended my father's funeral to show my respect, but I also had an ulterior motive. I wanted to be a witness to my family. The man who offered the eulogy was a man I grew up calling "Uncle Dutch." In reality, he was my dad's best friend from his high school days. Dad actually helped him break into the wrestling business, and he wrestled as Dutch Savage. He became very well known, but I just knew him as Uncle Dutch. At the funeral, I approached him and began to share the gospel with him.

Uncle Dutch told me, "Carl, you know, your parents' divorce was probably the best thing that could have ever happened to you." I knew he was right, but his comment still hurt me deeply. I had desperately desired a close relationship with my father, and I didn't want my parents to divorce. I never wanted to be forced to choose between my dad and my mom. Kids should never have to make that choice. I wanted to be with my father, too, but I couldn't.

As I talked with my mom at the funeral, she told me, "Carl, you know what your dad's greatest desire was? When you turned sixteen, he was going to pull you out of school and take you on the road with him. He wanted to help you break into the wrestling business. And you guys were going to wrestle as the 'New Kentuckians' and relive his glory days."

I left the funeral very confused and sad. I praise God for my sweet wife, Masami. She truly loved on me while I went through this difficult time in my life. She is such a blessing in my life, and helps me to keep my eyes and heart focused on the Lord and not on my circumstances.

How I Almost Ended Up as a "New Kentuckian"

My father's so-called "glory days" happened when he was the younger half of the famous wrestling duo called "The Kentuckians." In the sixties, the Kentuckians set attendance records all over the United States. For example, they were the first sporting event ever to sell out the large Charlotte auditorium in North Carolina. I was told that a state patrolman said they had to turn away between 3,000 and 5,000 people because the event had sold out. The line of traffic supposedly backed up almost three miles from the auditorium into the city.

Back then, my dad seemed to have it all—at least in the world's eyes. He had fame and glory, and from time to time, a lot of money. But when he passed away, he had next to nothing. He had been living in a $3,000 trailer (one that he hadn't even paid for yet) and worked taking tolls in a toll booth. (I mean no disrespect to anyone's profession. I've had a number of jobs in my life, from shearing sheep to shoveling coal. The Lord carefully places each of us in a variety of environments to be His witnesses. I'm just sharing that the circumstances had

"The Kentuckians": Luke Brown and Jake Smith

changed drastically in his life. At one point he had all the material things the world could offer, but then he lost it all.)

I want to emphasize again that if you sell out for what the world can give you, the world can, and often will, take it away. When you sell out for the Lord Jesus Christ, though, nothing can take you out of His hand. What a contrast!

After my dad had passed away, I went back to his house and found that he had very little in the way of possessions. The only thing that I was given after his funeral was an old windbreaker he wore while working at the toll booth.

BIG LUKE BROWN

"Big Luke Brown" trading card

Requiem for a Heavyweight cast: Anthony Quinn (in jacket), Micky Rooney (hat), my father (far right)

I went on eBay after the funeral to see if I could find any memorabilia that would give me something to remember about my dad. I was amazed to find all kinds of cool things. I bought magazines, posters, and even a video of a movie he appeared in entitled *Requiem for a Heavyweight* with Oscar winner Anthony Quinn.

My son, Dennis, was thirteen at the time of his grandfather's passing (the same age I was when my parents divorced). He looked at all that memorabilia and said, "Dad, wrestling's cool, isn't it?" Oh, man! My heart fell right through the floor. (By the way, this was probably the second scariest moment of my life! I had thought the same thing when I was his age, and I didn't want my son going in that direction.) The last thing I want to do is glamorize and popularize professional wrestling. It's a sick business. Believe me, I know; I've been around it. I know who and what's involved in it.

I told him, "The five minutes of fame isn't worth the life-time of sorrow that you really get in the long run. No, it's not cool at all."

To illustrate this to Dennis, I did something that I wouldn't necessarily suggest others do. I took him to watch a documentary titled *Beyond the Mat*. In this documentary, the producers did a good job of revealing what it was really like behind the scenes in wrestling. They showed young men trying to break into the wrestling business, as well as wrestlers in their prime, and even one guy who was extremely famous at one time but who now was past his prime. That man was Jake "The Snake" Roberts.

One clip showed Jake in his prime, wrestling in front of 65,000 people. He had money and fame. He even had his own T-shirts and action figure. Then the movie showed where they had caught up with him in 1999: wrestling in North Platte, Nebraska, in front of a crowd of no more than a hundred and fifty people. Jake was not looking healthy. Obviously, he had been using drugs, and he clearly was not a happy person. He had no relationship with his ex-wives, and no relationship with his children. In fact, in the film, Jake is shown walking in a room to talk with his daughter. According to the film he hadn't seen her in two and a half years. After spending five minutes with her, he walked out of the room and left her standing there. That was it!

In the movie theater, tears ran down my face as I sat there with my son. A number of people sitting around us probably thought I was crazy—this big guy bawling at a wrestling movie! But my children are precious to me, and to watch Jake spend five minutes with his daughter and then walk out just broke my heart.

Then the film showed Jake with his father. In the director's commentary, there was one comment that cut me to the bone.

The director said that Jake was with his father for about three hours while they were filming, but they never once looked each other in the eyes, and they never once talked to each other.

I was in tears again. Jake's dad was right there, and he didn't have a relationship with him. Yet I desperately desired a relationship with my dad, and I didn't have a chance to spend time with him. To be honest, I was mad. I'm not saying that my response was correct, but it's how I felt! I so desperately wanted a relationship with my father, but I couldn't get it. The fact that Jake's dad was right there yet they didn't have a relationship just broke my heart.

When Dennis and I walked out of that theater, he looked at me and said, "Dad, God's been good to you, hasn't He?" Thankfully, he got the message. Wrestling wasn't that cool after all.

THE DIFFERENCE A DECISION MAKES

This whole encounter caused me to reflect on my life and what God had done to deliver me. The words of Uncle Dutch and my mother at the funeral stuck in my mind. I realized how God had used the broken pieces and difficult circumstances of my life to prepare me to be willing and able to serve Him. One of those circumstances was my decision at age thirteen to stay with my mom.

I didn't recognize how right that decision was until about six months after my father's death. I was thirty-six then; twenty-three years had passed since the day I had spent with my father, in tears, telling him I wanted to stay with my mother. A friend of mine contacted me and said, "Carl, you've got to get this photo off eBay." When I saw the photo, it brought everything together. I call it my "Paul Harvey, Rest of the Story" moment. (You *mature* folks know what I'm talking about!) It's

The New Kentuckians: My father, "Big Luke Brown"
(top), and Jake "The Snake" Roberts (bottom)

a photo of the "New Kentuckians." It showed my father with his new tag team partner—the person he had "broken into" the wrestling business instead of me.

I remembered my mom saying that my dad's greatest desire was to take me on the road with him when I was sixteen so we could wrestle as the New Kentuckians. I was looking at a picture that I fully believe would have been me if I had made a different decision when I was thirteen and my dad had asked me to come and live with him.

What made it even more *personal* was who his tag team partner was. It was the man who later wrestled as Jake "The Snake" Roberts. Remember the film I took my son to see that

The Kentuckians: Jake Smith, father of
Jake "The Snake" Roberts (top), and
Luke Brown, my dad (bottom)

showed the behind-the-scenes world of professional wrestling?
He was one of the men the movie had spotlighted.

What made it even more *powerful* was the fact that Jake's
father and my father also wrestled together. That's when they
had all their fame and all their glory. Jake's dad (the man in
the documentary, whom Jake didn't even speak to) and my
father had wrestled as the Kentuckians.

Here's the real shocker: I grew up around Jake "The Snake"
Roberts. In fact, his father (who recently passed away) had
changed my diapers. When I grew older, I played at his house
with him and his brother, Mike (who later wrestled as Sam
Houston).

When I saw that picture of the New Kentuckians, I was flabbergasted. I realized that the person in the photo was supposed to be *me*. And there is no doubt in my mind that it would have been me if I had stayed with my father. Wrestling would have been the only life I knew. There is only one reason I wasn't there: the decision I made at age thirteen to stay with my mother instead of going to live with my dad. I believe that was why the Holy Spirit filled me with such fear when Dad asked me to go live with him when I was a boy.

MY FATHER'S PLAN

You see, my earthly father had a plan for my life, as most of our earthly parents do. But that may or may not fit with what God has called us to do. Your heavenly Father, who loves you more than you will ever understand this side of heaven, also has a good and perfect plan for your life.

When I saw that picture of the New Kentuckians, I was flabbergasted. I realized that the person in the photo was supposed to be me. Wrestling would have been the only life I knew.

Another truth hit me as I looked at that picture. Even *if* I had gone down that road, Jesus would have still loved me and His gift of salvation would have still been offered to me. It's offered to everyone, regardless of their path in life. I know what the stones and boulders have been in my life on the path I chose, but I sometimes wonder what obstacles I would have had to overcome had I taken another path. Would it have been more difficult for me to come to a saving knowledge of Jesus Christ? I'll never know. What I do know is that He was guiding me, even before I came to know Him, and I am so thankful to Him for that.

Almost every day now, I tell young people that their decisions have consequences. Some are short-term, some are long-term, and, sadly, some last for a hopeless eternity without Christ. What I feel called to do is to help non-Christians to understand how they can trust in Christ and receive the gift of eternal life. And, to help Christians know that they can trust the Word of God completely.

Christian, because the Bible deals with everything, from family issues to key questions about creation, life, death, etc., we can *know* how to handle all the struggles that we face. Jesus will guide and direct our lives when we follow His instructions. Have you made the decision to trust God's Word completely in all areas of your life? If not, I hope you will feel compelled to do that today.

I want to give you one more verse to keep in mind: "For everyone to whom much is given, from him much will be required" (Luke 12:48). All of us, whether we realize it or not, have been given "much." If you are reading this book, then I know that, at a minimum, you've been given the gifts of life, sight, and intelligence. Most likely, you've had enough education to get you through life. You very likely have at least one parent or guardian who loves you. You probably have a job, or some way to keep a roof over your head, and you have food on your table every day.

Christian, God has given us so "much" more! He's given you eternal life and equipped you to serve Him. Are you using your life to bring "much" glory to God and are you staying focused on His will and His way? Much will be required of us one day when we give account of how we used the gifts that God so freely gave to us.

Non-Christian, no matter your background, your circumstances, or your place in life, God has also given "much" to you and for you. God sent His Son, Jesus Christ, to pay the penalty for your sin.

Have you ever told a lie or taken anything that didn't belong to you? Of course, you have; we all have. Then you have broken two of the Ten Commandments, God's moral Law. That makes you a liar and a thief—a lawbreaker (sinner) in God's eyes. In a court of law you'd be found guilty of breaking the law and sentenced to pay a fine or go to jail. The Bible tells us that the fine for breaking the Law of God is the death penalty: "For the wages of sin is death..." (Romans 6:23). But God provided a way for your case to be dismissed. He sent His Son, Jesus Christ, to be born as a man and die in your place. Jesus was righteous before God and lived a sinless life. When He hung on the cross, Jesus took upon Himself your sins and died to pay the penalty for them so that you can be forgiven. He then rose from the dead and offers eternal life to those who repent and trust in Him. This is the gift of God, freely given.

> For by grace you have been saved through faith, and that not of yourselves; it is the gift of God, not of works, lest anyone should boast. (Ephesians 2:8,9)

In order to receive this gift you must understand that you are *a sinner in need of forgiveness*. You must understand that *Jesus took on your sins and paid the penalty for them on the cross*. And, in exchange, He offers you His righteousness (right standing before God). This is called the great exchange.

John 3:16,17 says, "For God so loved the world that He gave His only begotten Son, that whoever believes in Him should not perish but have everlasting life. For God did not send His Son into the world to condemn the world, but that the world through Him might be saved."

Never think that you're beyond His reach. I strayed far from the Lord in my younger years, but as I've testified in this book, He loved me and saved me. All you need to do in order to receive God's gift of forgiveness and eternal life is:

Pray to Him and ask Him to forgive your sins.

Repent (turn from your sins), and tell Him that you understand you are a sinner in need of a Savior (you can even name your sins; He already knows them anyway).

Trust in what Jesus Christ did on the cross to pay the penalty for your sins.

Repent and trust in Jesus Christ alone for your salvation. He loves you and He promises that He will save you if you call upon Him (Romans 10:13). First Timothy 1:15 tells us, "This is a faithful saying and worthy of all acceptance, that Christ Jesus came into the world to save sinners..."

> *Never think that you're beyond His reach. I strayed far from the Lord in my younger years, but as I've testified in this book, He loved me and saved me.*

Non-Christian, you've just read the gospel message. If you have turned from your sins, asked God for forgiveness, and placed your trust in Jesus Christ, we'd love to hear from you. Please contact us at Reasons for Hope (www.rforh.com, saved@rforh.com) and tell us your story. We have a gift we'd like to send you.

If the gospel still doesn't make sense to you, or you are unwilling to turn to Christ and receive His gift, we'd love to hear from you also. Perhaps we can answer any questions and objections you may have. Please write to us as well, at hope@rforh.com.

■ ■ ■

As I began to get more involved in creation ministry and learn more about the Bible, by God's grace, I became better equipped to minister to people. I started to feel more confident sharing my hope in Christ with others as I discovered how to use the Bible to overcome people's most common questions and objections to the gospel. As a new Christian, I had been profoundly awestruck by the pilot who shared the truths from Scripture about creation, giving me the answers I sought. In Part 3, I want to do the same for you so that you will be equipped to have similar conversations with non-Christians or Christians who may have questions about evolution, suffering, dinosaurs, absolute truth, and other topics. I hope addressing these questions will be helpful to you, whether you're the one asking, or the one desiring to answer.

PART THREE

Answering
COMMON OBJECTIONS
to the Christian Faith

13

What About the Problem of Pain, Suffering, and Death?

T hrough my travels and speaking engagements, I discovered that Christians as well as non-Christians were asking me all sorts of questions on a variety of topics. Many of their questions were about issues they were facing in their everyday lives, but they were unable to find satisfactory answers to them. As I was asked about these topics, I was forced to get into the Word of God and study so that I could offer people answers from a biblical perspective. Remember, 1 Peter 3:15 is not a suggestion but a command: we should *all* be able to give an answer to *every* person who asks us about our faith. God provides each of us countless opportunities to share the reasons for our hope with people around us, whether neighbors, strangers, friends, or family, and we want to be ready.

Even my wife had been asking me a lot of the same probing questions that I was hearing on the road, especially about the book of Genesis. Although she was a Christian, Masami had numerous questions as a result of her polytheistic culture and background. One of the issues she sought an answer to was this: "If God is loving and good, why does He allow pain, suffering, and death?"

The question about the problem of pain is one of the primary objections that people raise to the gospel. Tsunamis, murders, bridge collapses, terrorist attacks, wars—every time we turn on the TV or pick up the newspaper, we see stories of pain, suffering, death, and destruction. Our culture's obsession with media has brought home to us the reality of death and suffering that occurs all over the world. As a result, many Americans are plagued by this age-old question: how could there be a God of love when the earth is filled with so much suffering and death?

A FALSE VIEW OF HISTORY

I was on the board of directors for Answers in Genesis when the attacks on the World Trade Center took place on September 11, 2001. Right after 9/11 one of our staff members interviewed a New York City police officer who told us that people were desperate for answers. But, the officer said, people had the wrong "big picture" to understand such events because they had a false view of history. By that he meant that people had been taught in school that, through the process of evolution, millions of years of death and suffering had occurred before man even appeared on the earth.

The officer told us that he believed people really needed the true picture of history—the one found in Genesis—to understand death and suffering. According to the Bible, God made a perfect world inhabited by perfect humans, which He pronounced "very good." But Adam and Eve's rebellion (recorded in Genesis 3) brought sin and death into the world and brought a curse on all creation.

That is the key to helping people deal with the problem of pain, suffering, and death. God gave us perfection. He never meant for us to have to experience suffering and death. He created Adam and Eve to live in perfect fellowship with Him in the Garden of Eden. Death is actually our enemy. It doesn't belong here. Adam "let it in," so to speak, when he rebelled against God. Now, because of his sin, we are all born spiritually dead, without God's Holy Spirit.

In addition, each of us purposely chooses to sin. Because we have sin on our record (both the sin imputed to us through Adam and our own sinful choices), we have to face the penalty of that sin, which God says is death and eternity in hell (Romans 6:23; Revelation 21:8).

But there is good news. This good news is Jesus Christ. God loves us so much that, as soon as sin and death invaded creation (Genesis 3), He provided a way for us to be rescued from that sin and death so we can have eternal life with Him. His first promise of a coming Savior, a Redeemer to free us, is found in Genesis 3:15: "And I will put enmity between you and the woman, and between your seed and her Seed; He shall bruise your head, and you shall bruise His heel." This promise was fulfilled in His Son, Jesus, who came into the world over two thousand years ago to die on the cross to pay the penalty for our sins, then rose from the dead to conquer death on our behalf. He died to redeem man, and one day He will create a new heaven and a new earth where there will be no more curse—no more sin, no suffering, sorrow, or death (Revelation 21:1–4; 22:3).

So how can a loving God allow suffering and death? He allows it as the consequence of Adam's sin and our sin. It wasn't part of His original plan for people, and though it grieves Him when we suffer hurt, pain, and loss, they will continue until Jesus returns and restores all creation to God's perfect plan. So rather than blaming God, we should be blaming mankind. What's more, we should gratefully accept God's gracious offer to rescue us, to save us by the precious blood of His Son. Second Peter 3:9 says, "The Lord is not slack concerning His promise, as some count slackness, but is longsuffering toward us, not willing that any should perish but that all should come to repentance."

A HEART CONDITION

Let me share with you a personal story that gives a practical way to deal with suffering. When I first reported to Chicago O'Hare as a controller, I met one Christian coworker who was very bold about his faith. Roger and I hit it off immediately, and I really valued our friendship, even though he did things to challenge me and "get me going" at times.

He knew my creation science background, and on more than one occasion, Roger would set the stage for a witnessing opportunity. When he saw me having lunch with a group of controllers, he would walk up and ask, "Carl, what do you mean that *Jurassic Park* proves that dinosaurs aren't millions of years old?" or "Hey, did you hear they proved there was a global flood on Mars?" The other guys were very curious and skeptical, so they'd immediately start asking me a bunch of questions. Roger would just walk off smiling!

Roger also got me involved with the rest of the guys by inviting me to play softball with them. He was well respected by everyone, so the fact that he reached out to me when I was new got the others to accept me as well. It was a pretty difficult place if you didn't party with the guys. Roger had been there for a while so they had already accepted him.

One night I was working on a new sermon entitled "You Have a Heart Condition," using James 4:14 as the key verse. This verse says, "You do not know what will happen tomorrow. For what is your life? It is even a vapor that appears for a little time and then vanishes away."

In the sermon, I was planning to ask folks to imagine walking into their doctor's office for an annual checkup. He asks how you're feeling. You tell him, "Not too bad. I'm a little tired, more than usual, but there's a lot going on at work so that's probably why. Overall, though, I'm doing pretty well." He examines you and sends you to have blood tests done.

When you get a phone call from him on the following day, you know something is out of whack. So you ask him, "What's up?"

"Well," he says, "I'm sorry to have to tell you this, but you've got a heart condition. I don't know how long you have left: it could be a year, a week, a day, or even just an hour. I'm not sure. And, unfortunately, there's nothing that you or I can do about it!"

If you ever received a wake-up call like that, what would it do to change your lifestyle? Honestly, I believe that you and I would quickly make some vital lifestyle changes, and they would be no problem for us. Eat healthy? Exercise every day? No problem. Lose weight? Sure thing. Slow down and lower our stress levels? Of course. We would do all of these things if we thought they could stave off the inevitable for a while.

I wanted to end my sermon with this: "I'm not a doctor, but let me tell you, you do have a serious heart condition—it's called sin. I don't know how long you've got left to live; it could be a year, a week, a day, or even just an hour. The good news is that you can do something about it! That something is to receive the gift of eternal life from God, the Creator of life." And then I would present the gospel message.

The following morning the sermon I was developing was still fresh in my mind, and I was trying to come up with real-life illustrations to make its message more relevant. I clearly remember that day when I arrived at work for my ATC shift and saw a message posted at the sign-in log: "Roger died last night. He had a heart attack at the softball game." The message then listed the information for his funeral. Roger left behind a wife and two young children. Although he was only thirty-eight, his time was up. Do you think he expected that to be his last day? No. He didn't even know he had a heart problem. I learned that he had what is called the "widow maker," and even with immediate medical attention he would have still died. There was nothing anyone could do. None of us know when we'll take our last breath on this earth, but when we do we'll meet our Maker and we'd better be prepared. Roger belonged to Jesus Christ and he was ready to go be with Him. Are you?

None of us know when we'll take our last breath on this earth, but when we do we'll meet our Maker and we'd better be prepared. Are you?

Fast forward a few years: I was visiting a Christian friend of mine who is a cardiologist (heart doctor) in the Pittsburgh area, and he asked if I'd like to go with him on his rounds at the hospital. Of course I said, "Yes!" How cool is that?!

As we walked into the hospital, the nurses saw Dr. John and ran up to him with charts. One nurse asked me, "Are you studying to be a heart surgeon?"

"No," I joked, "but I stayed at a Holiday Inn Express last night!" She laughed and then told me, "You'd better get your roller skates on! Dr. John is the best. He's the first one in and the last one out!"

What an amazing way for a Christian to be described by his peers in a secular environment. I could tell that everyone had such great respect for Dr. John. And this was not a Christian hospital. This really made me want to challenge Christians to step up and be the best, no matter what we do. Regardless of our vocation, we still represent Christ!

As I accompanied him on his rounds, Dr. John would pray with his patients. If they weren't Christians, he would offer them gospel tracts. It was unbelievable to see this doctor offer so much care and such spiritual boldness among folks with serious health conditions.

At one point we walked into a room where nurses put a lead vest on me and a hair net on my head. Dr. John washed up and I followed him into the operating room. Talk about being in the Twilight Zone! The man on the table was awake, and he looked a lot like me. One of the nurses asked me if I was studying to be a heart doctor.

"No, I'm with him!" I said, pointing to Dr. John. I didn't want to wear out my "Holiday Inn Express" line!

Dr. John started to perform a procedure in which he inserted a tiny video camera and threaded it up the artery in the leg to the heart. He explained everything as I watched it all on the monitor. It was amazing!

Next we went into the ER. As we entered a room where an elderly man sat at his wife's bedside, the man stood up to shake Dr. John's hand. I'm not a doctor by any means, but one look at this dear lady lying in the hospital bed told me that things weren't right!

Dr. John explained the situation to the man. It wasn't good. After some conversation, he asked the man if he could pray for them. The man said yes, and Dr. John gave me the privilege of praying for the man and his dear wife.

As we were leaving, the nurse asked Dr. John what he would like her to do for the patient. He said, "Put her on comfort measures."

Once we were in the hallway I asked, "Dr. John, what are 'comfort measures'?"

He said, "That's what we offer when there is nothing left I can do for her, Carl, except keep her comfortable until the Lord calls her home."

I felt as if I had been slapped. I stopped short right there in the middle of the hallway and said, "Dr. John, that's what I see in the world around me! That's what I see in so many churches. People are on 'comfort measures,' just trying to be comfortable until the Lord calls them home."

I paused before asking, "And what's the opposite of 'comfort measures'?"

"Full code," he said. "When we go 'full code,' we do everything we can to keep the patient alive."

Wow! We need to go "full code" when we see lost and dying people all around us.

My friends, the problem of pain and suffering is a real issue. We cannot minimize it. As you have seen in this chapter, there are clear and biblical answers to why and how death and suffering entered the world. They are not God's fault; they are our fault. But my question is, what are you going to do about it? Are you just going to keep your mouth shut and stay on "comfort measures"? Or will you go "full code" and seize every opportunity to share the gospel of Christ? That is the *only* thing that will give people true hope and eternal life.

> *There are clear, biblical answers to why and how death and suffering entered the world. They are not God's fault; they are our fault. But my question is, what are you going to do about it?*

What About Evolution?

A nother huge issue for many people today relates to man's origins. Like countless others who have been influenced by Darwin, Masami wondered, "How does the theory of evolution fit in with the Bible? Did God use the process of evolution to create everything?"

The theory of evolution asserts that all life forms (plants, animals, humans) began from a simple living cell, and through random mutations over millions of years, gradually became more complex. According to this theory, primitive "people" (called hominids) existed in an ape-like form for millions of years before the first humans appeared. Many Christians try to fit this theory into the biblical account of creation, but there are major problems with accepting the argument that God used evolution. We'll address just a few of them here.

First, if there was life in the world for millions of years before Adam, then there was death in the world before Adam was created. And if there was death before Adam was created, then there was sin also, for the Bible tells us that "the wages of sin is death" (Romans 6:23). It would also mean that the Bible is incorrect when it says that "through one man [Adam] sin entered the world, and death through sin" (Romans 5:12) and "by man came death" (1 Corinthians 15:21). If we accept the teaching of millions of years and try to "fit" it into the Bible, we must accept sin and death in the world before Adam. The reality is that by trying to put long ages in the biblical account so the Bible will "fit" with science, we actually are attacking the character of God! Christian, we can't do that. When God told us that death came into the world as a consequence of man's actions, He meant it. And He tells us that it entered by one man, Adam.

Now, many will try to argue that this "death" pertains only to humans and that those who inhabited the earth before Adam were non-humans (primitive, ape-like hominids). Since they weren't human, they could supposedly die and not cause a conflict with the Bible. Sorry, Romans 8:22 states that the whole of creation—not just humans—groans and suffers *because of sin*.

Another attempt to get around the literal reading of Romans 5:12, that death came as a result of man's sin, is to claim that the death spoken of was only a spiritual death. Sorry, wrong again. Although Adam and Eve didn't physically die the moment they sinned, physical death came into the world at that time as a direct consequence of their sin. God said, "For out of it [the ground] you were taken; for dust you are, and to dust you shall return" (Genesis 3:19). If Adam and Eve had not disobeyed God and eaten the forbidden fruit, they would have remained in the Garden of Eden, partaking of the Tree of Life, and physical death would not have entered the world.

Last, but not least—this one gets strange—there are those who say that the ape-like creatures (hominids) that supposedly existed prior to humans didn't have souls, since only humans have souls. In their mind, this would allow the theory of evolution to be combined with biblical creation—where death occurred over millions of years as life evolved, then at a certain point God intervened and created the first man, Adam, where we pick up the Genesis account. Now, I'm not sure where they get that from, but there is nothing scriptural or scientific to support that thinking. Furthermore, this would present a situation where God created a pre-Adamic world that suffered sin and death, but provided no means of redemption. Again, there's nothing to support any of this. It's just conjecture from those who don't want to believe God's Word.

These questions were a huge issue for my wife. She believed the Bible, but because she had been raised in Japan where the schools and media heavily promoted the concept of evolution over millions of years as a fact, she was perplexed.

So starting from the Scriptures, acknowledging it as the authority in life, I tried giving Masami the answers she sought about creation and evolution. At one point she asked me, "Are you saying I'm not a Christian because I don't believe like you?"

"No, I'm not saying that," I told her. As I mentioned previously, this was not the case. Masami had given her life to Christ even before I did. But she had not yet learned to trust the Scriptures completely.

Thinking back on that incident now, I've seen time and time again that Christians can be inconsistent in how they view the Bible and, of course, still be Christian. Unfortunately, we're often taught, even in the church, to approach God's Word with this mindset: "God, I know what You wrote, but let me tell You what You meant! I know that You said You created Adam and Eve *in the beginning*, but because You didn't quite understand science, I'll help you out on this issue. Since science has proven that the earth is millions of years old and man has evolved from a common ancestor of the ape, we *know* there must have been hominids who lived and died for hundreds of thousands of years before Adam. And this pre-Adamic race of men must have been soulless."

Sounds like the Let's Help God Society (which has a lot of members). Friends, when people start adding man's wisdom to God's Word, that's exactly what they're doing—trying to help out God. Those who want to add a "gap" of time between Genesis 1 and 2 to account for the "fact" that the earth is millions of years old are telling God He doesn't know what happened in the past. The Word of God doesn't allow for a "gap" of millions of years, during which evolutionary processes took place.

Some people argue that the six days of creation in Genesis 1 don't have to be literal 24-hour days because "a verse, somewhere in the New Testament, says that a day is like a thousand years." If this is the case, they argue, then the "days" in Genesis can be long periods of time.

The answer to this claim is that the verse they're thinking of, 2 Peter 3:8, has nothing to do with the days in Genesis. The verse says that *"with the Lord* one day is as a thousand years, *and* a thousand years as one day"* (emphasis added). Remember, we don't want to be guilty of "prooftexting" by ignoring the surrounding verses that explain the writer's intent. In context, this verse is stating that, since God created earthly time, He therefore exists outside the dimension of time and is not bound by time. That's why it says "with the Lord"—meaning from His perspective, outside of time—a thousand years and a day are the same. Likewise, Psalm 90:4 tells us, "For in Your sight a thousand years are like yesterday that passes by, like a few hours of the night."

Those who try to make the days of creation more than a 24-hour day would never say that, according to 2 Peter 3:8, the three days from the cross to the resurrection were equal to three thousand years. In addition, they ignore the second part of the verse. They would never say that the (approximately) two-thousand-year period from Abraham to the cross was only two days. The bottom line is that they have taken the verse out of context to try to make it say what they want it to say, as a way to fit "science" into the Bible.

Furthermore, the Hebrew word used for "day" in Genesis 1 is *yom*. It is used 2,301 times in the Old Testament alone. Outside of Genesis, when the word *yom* is used:

- with a number (410 times), it always means an ordinary 24-hour day

- with "evening" and "morning" (38 times), it always means an ordinary 24-hour day

- with "evening" or "morning" (27 times), it always means an ordinary 24-hour day

- with "night" (52 times), it always means an ordinary 24-hour day

Why would Genesis 1 be an exception?

Finally, the Scripture is abundantly clear that the days in Genesis are the same length as we know days to be today. God used the seven days of creation to be a pattern for how man would use time:

> "For in six days the LORD made the heavens and the earth, the sea, and all that is in them, and rested the seventh day. Therefore the LORD blessed the Sabbath day and hallowed it." (Exodus 20:11)

TRUSTING SCRIPTURE

The point is this: when we start adding our opinions to God's Word to tell Him what He meant, we're elevating our wisdom above God's Word. As Christians, we need to make a decision about who we are going to allow to be our authority. Either man and his fallible opinion, or God and His holy, infallible Word. Joshua 24:15 says:

> "But if it seems evil to you to serve the LORD, choose for yourselves this day whom you will serve, whether the gods which your fathers served that were on the other side of the River, or the gods of the Amorites, in whose land you dwell. But as for me and my house, we will serve the LORD."

Make a choice, Christian. If you are struggling with something as simple as the days in Genesis, may I offer this. As Christians, we are followers of Jesus Christ. He is the Son of God, our King, our Master, our Savior. Jesus quoted Genesis twenty-five times. He accepted Genesis as real history. If Jesus can take it that way, I sure can.

As Christians, we need to make a decision about who we are going to allow to be our authority. Either man and his fallible opinion, or God and His holy, infallible Word.

Imagine this: you die and find yourself, facedown on the ground, at the feet of Jesus. He asks you, "What were you thinking? How in the world could you believe that the days in Genesis weren't exactly what I said—days? How could you believe there were millions of years of death and suffering before Adam was created? What were you thinking?" You could respond, "My God, science said...!"

Let's try that again. You find yourself facedown in front of Jesus. He says, "What were you thinking? How could you believe that I created in six 'real' 24-hour days? How could you believe that I made the world perfect and it was Adam's sin that brought death to My creation? How could you believe that?" Because I hold the Scriptures to be true, I know I would respond, "My God, Your Word said..."

Choose you this day whom *you* will follow, but as for me and my household, we're standing on every word the Lord has given us, even if we don't have full understanding.

Why do we fall for the trap of elevating man's wisdom above God's Word? I believe the problem is due in large part to our education in the secular school system. (Let's be honest: our schools are not "public" schools. They are secular schools that teach philosophies of secular humanism. Christians make up a big portion of the "public" schools, but we are not allowed to share our beliefs in the "public" school environment.)

Many Christians therefore take what they believe has been proven by "science" (evolution) and try to make it fit into the timeline of the Bible, although they don't do that with other biblical teachings. For example, many times good church folks tell me that they just can't believe in a young earth because "science has proven the earth is millions of years old!" They'll tell me to just give people the Gospel of John. My response is, "If I can't trust Genesis, why should I give them John? Either they're both true or they're both not true!"

If we can't trust what our eternal, omniscient God has told us about the days in Genesis because we need modern "science" to give us "proof," then we definitely can't trust the virgin birth or the resurrection, because "science" has proven that neither of those is possible either! Masami and I have learned that whatever the topic, we should look to God's Word first for answers, and trust what He says, rather than looking to fallible men and their erroneous science for so-called proof.

As Masami studied and learned more about Scripture, her thinking began to change. The day that she chose to embrace a comprehensive respect for the authority of Scripture was a special day for me. It was a humorous incident with our son that was the catalyst to help her realize just how important it is to trust God's Word completely. Masami had told Dennis, who was seven at the time, to go take a shower. Like many boys that age, he really didn't care for taking showers, so he just went into the bathroom and splashed some water from the sink on his hair. As he left the bathroom to go to his room, Masami confronted him. She knew what he had done.

"You didn't take a shower, did you?" she asked.

He immediately burst into tears and said, "It's not my fault, Mom! It's because of Adam's sin!"

When I heard this, I sat Dennis down and had a serious talk with him. "What you just did was what Adam did when God confronted him for his sin," I gently told him. "Adam blamed someone else for his own bad choices." It was a touching experience as, through his tears, he sincerely apologized. Now an adult, he still has a very sensitive spirit and is serious about his faith in God. I cannot think of a time when I have ever questioned him telling us the truth since that day. He must have learned his lesson!

This event really stuck in Masami's mind. She knew that I was teaching our children that the Bible's history and principles were true, and it was obvious that they truly believed it. If they could believe the Bible when it talked about Adam's sin being a real event, shouldn't they believe the passages that tell how God created the world? Masami began to realize that we couldn't just pick and choose what we want to believe from the Bible. Either the entire Bible is true, or none of it is true.

Shortly after that incident, Masami came up to me and remarked, "I understand now why you trust the Bible this way. It makes the Bible so easy! God said it so I believe it." Masami then told me she was glad to see me more involved in creation ministry, and today, she completely supports me and encourages me in ministry.

15

What About Dinosaurs?

A fascination of many young people in my speaking audiences, and a topic that bothered Masami, is this: "Why doesn't the Bible mention dinosaurs?"

I suggest that it does! Now, it's true that we don't find the word "dinosaur" in the Bible, but we shouldn't expect to because it's a relatively new word. The word *dinosauria*, meaning "terrible lizard," was coined in 1841 by Sir Richard Owen.

To show how new the word is, I encourage folks to look at the 1828 Noah Webster dictionary, because they may be surprised by what they find. Words like "rocket," "computer," "locomotive," and "jet" are included—though the meanings may be different—but "dinosaur" is not even there.

The King James version of the Bible, one of the earliest English translations, was published in 1611, more than two centuries before the word "dinosaur" was created. So while "dinosaur" wasn't around when the Bible was translated into English, another word used several times in the Bible may give us an answer. It's the Hebrew word *tanniyn*, often translated "dragon."

The clearest example of how these animals (referred to in Scripture as "dragon," "behemoth," or "Leviathan") could easily be what we know today as dinosaurs is found in Job 40:15–24. There we read about a creature called *behemoth*, which was one of the largest land animals God ever created:

> "Look now at the behemoth, which I made along with you;
> He eats grass like an ox.
>
> See now, his strength is in his hips,
> And his power is in his stomach muscles.
>
> He moves his tail like a cedar;
> The sinews of his thighs are tightly knit.
>
> His bones are like beams of bronze,
> His ribs like bars of iron.
>
> He is the first of the ways of God;
> Only He who made him can bring near His sword.
>
> Surely the mountains yield food for him,
> And all the beasts of the field play there.
>
> He lies under the lotus trees,
> In a covert of reeds and marsh.
>
> The lotus trees cover him with their shade;
> The willows by the brook surround him.
>
> Indeed the river may rage,
> Yet he is not disturbed;
> He is confident, though the Jordan gushes into his mouth,
>
> Though he takes it in his eyes,
> Or one pierces his nose with a snare."

This creature ate grass like an ox. (Evidence indicates sauropod dinosaurs did also.) It was huge and powerful, with an enormous tail. (Archaeological digs have produced evidence sauropod dinosaurs were also.) In fact, this animal was so big that it could drink safely from the Jordan River even at flood stage. (The sauropod dinosaurs were big enough to do that.) Its bones were strong, as though fortified with bronze and iron. (Fossils indicate the strength of sauropod bones.) And this animal was difficult, if not impossible, to capture or trap. (I doubt there were dinosaur trappers back then; could you imagine the size of those traps?)

In this passage, it certainly sounds like God is describing what we would now call a sauropod dinosaur. The one fact that makes it almost undeniable is that this animal had a tail like a cedar (verse 17). Many Bible commentators will suggest that this creature may be a hippopotamus or an elephant. Hmm...ever seen the tails of these animals? They aren't huge, I can tell you that!

The first time I read that this creature "moves his tail like a cedar" (verse 17), I thought of two experiences I had growing up. The first experience was the worst job I ever had and, at the time, my only experience with cedar trees. When I was a high school senior, I did a lot of farm work. On one occasion I got paid two dollars an hour to walk the hills of Virginia with pruning shears, cutting down juvenile cedar trees so they wouldn't get caught up in the hay combine. At the end of the day, I couldn't even stand up straight. It was horrible!

My second experience with cedar trees took place in Japan while I was on a speaking tour there many years later. Driving through the mountains, I saw trees that were so big that I couldn't wrap my arms around them, so tall that when I stood at their base I couldn't even see the top of the tree. I asked my driver what kind of trees they were. He responded, "Cedar trees!"

I immediately thought of Job 40:17. The description in the Bible does *not* fit the tail of any elephant or hippo I've ever seen, unless it was one of those scrawny little cedar trees I had cut down in high school—a little sapling. However, the tail of a sauropod dinosaur fits very well with the enormous cedar trees that I saw in Japan. And in biblical times, the mature cedars were large, beautiful trees. Scripture often refers to the "cedars of Lebanon," which were massive trees that were cut down to build enormous structures like temples and palaces.

When we look at the evidence for dinosaurs through the lens of biblical history, it truly isn't just fairytale. The fossil evidence that we see is consistent with what the Word of God teaches. When we allow God's Word to be our authority, we can answer other commonly asked questions about dinosaurs as well.

HOW DID THEY FIT ON THE ARK?

Another common question I am asked is: "How did Noah fit the dinosaurs on the ark?" First, we have to realize that in our culture, we have many misconceptions about dinosaurs. Due to movies like *Jurassic Park*, we have the false notion that all dinosaurs were gigantic animals. That's not what is found in the fossil record. Yes, there are large dinosaur fossils, but the reality is that dinosaurs came in all shapes and sizes. One of the smallest dinosaurs that ever lived was about the size of a Chihuahua.

Even the really big dinosaurs laid eggs, and the largest egg ever found was about 17 inches in length. That means that even the largest dinosaurs were small at one time! The Bible tells us that God brought the animals to Noah; Noah didn't have to go out and round them up (Genesis 6:20; 7:7–9). Why wouldn't God bring the younger ones, which would have been smaller? That only makes sense. I like to put it this way: If you're going to take people to repopulate a planet, you're not going to take me! I'm old and big; my repopulating days are done. You'd want to take my grandson to do that.

In addition, lizards continue to grow as long as they live. So I believe the fact that we find these very large animals supports what the Bible teaches. God originally created mankind to live forever. In the time of Adam and Eve, people lived much longer than they do today. (Methuselah, for example, lived for 969 years!) I would expect that the animals created alongside man lived for long ages as well. We should therefore find evidence of very large animals, which we do.

Another point to consider is how many of these animals were needed on the ark. There may be thousands of names of dinosaurs, but the truth is that, even according to National Geographic, fully one-third to one-half of all the dinosaurs we read about today never even existed![15] The fossil evidence is so poor that multiple names were given to the bones of the same animal that had already been found. Scientists are just now discovering that they may have a hundred bones of dinosaurs excavated from around the globe, but they are just different specimens of the same species. The reality is that there were probably fewer than one hundred different species of dinosaurs.

> *There may be thousands of names of dinosaurs, but the truth is that fully one-third to one-half of all the dinosaurs we read about today never even existed!*

Research has shown that, to allow for all the different species of animals we see today, the total number of animals needed on the ark is only about 8,000. Even if someone claimed the "required number" of animals taken on the ark was, say, 30,000, there still would have been plenty of room. The ark was enormous; Noah could have fit over 120,000 sheep-sized animals onto it. Most likely, the dinosaurs that went onto the ark were about the size of a sheep.

WHERE DID THEY GO?

Another related question that I often hear is: "If the dinosaurs went onto the ark, why don't we see them today?" I believe they did go onto the ark, because I have a record from someone who's always been there and knows everything: God. According to Genesis 7:14,15, two of every living creature (including dinosaurs) entered the ark so they could be preserved. I also believe there is evidence to support that they came off the ark. First, we have the mentions of "dragons" in Scripture. It's also significant that almost every culture has dragon legends. I'd suggest that these "legends" may in fact be based on actual encounters with animals like those we now call dinosaurs. Many times, the descriptions of the two creatures are very similar. The account we read of behemoth in Job 40 is such an example. And by the way, since Job lived after the flood, the animal described in Job must have been one that came off the ark and survived for a time.

Scientists have also discovered dinosaur bones that are not at all fossilized or mineralized. How could bones last 70 million years without rotting? That's just not possible. In addition, scientists have found what is thought to be dinosaur flesh, with blood vessels and red blood cells. This tissue could not possibly have lasted millions of years. If you ever hear of an account where DNA is found in anything that is supposedly millions of years old, you're actually hearing proof that it's not millions of years old! DNA breaks down by itself over time. Most scientists agree that DNA could not last more than about 100,000 years, and even that is only if it were cryogenically frozen and stored. Well, scientists are now purporting to have found DNA that is millions of years old? When one scientist was questioned about how DNA could last for so long, he said, "There must be some unknown process" that allows this to happen. How about this: it's not millions of years old!

To me, the reason we don't see dinosaurs today is simple. It's evident from the many descriptions in Scripture that the pre-flood and post-flood environments were radically different. Animals that thrived in the more protective, tropical environment of the pre-flood era may have struggled to survive after the flood. Large reptiles, for example, would have survived better in the tropical pre-flood environment. After the flood, they survived long enough to give rise to the dragon stories and the Job account, but eventually the dinosaurs died out as the atmosphere and living conditions on Earth changed.

This is just a start, but I hope this information about dinosaurs will help challenge your thinking about evolution and equip you to answer questions about these fascinating creatures. It's just another way that we can be prepared to offer people the reason for our hope and show them that God's Word does have an answer for everything!

Objection Overruled

A s I mentioned earlier, the newest generation, the Mosaics, have their own way of looking at the world. They are less linear in their thinking and are more likely to form their beliefs based on feelings and personal experiences rather than rational facts. Because they tend to embrace moral pragmatism, we have our work cut out for us to be able to answer their questions. We can share the hope that we have by always being ready when common objections about our faith and the gospel are raised. Let's take a look at some of these objections and think about the answers we can offer to overcome secular reasoning.

1) "THAT'S TRUE FOR YOU, BUT NOT FOR ME."

This thinking is called *relativism*. It's a philosophical position claiming that all points of view, no matter how strange or ridiculous, are equally valid. It implies that all moral positions and religious systems are true and that truth is relative to each individual. Relativism claims that there is no absolute truth and there are no right or wrong answers to anything. However, reality doesn't support this. For something to be absolute truth, it must be true in all cases and for all people. For example, in the natural world gravity exists. That's true for everyone. A person could say, "I *believe* gravity doesn't exist," but just having that belief doesn't make it true. Gravity still exists and the person is still governed by its laws.

Just claiming something is true, or untrue, doesn't make it so. It's a matter of determining the validity of the proof upon which the statement is made. If a statement is based on personal opinion, which is subjective, then it cannot be declared truth. Consider this. If I asked you if $2 + 4 = 6$, you'd say it was true. However, let's say I told you that I *believe* $2 + 4 = 5$; am I wrong? According to a relativist, I can't be wrong, because if I *believe* $2 + 4 = 5$ it's true for me, even if it's not true for you. What is "true" is determined by what I believe, not by whether it conforms to objective reality.

Do you see how silly and self-contradicting that thinking is? There certainly *are* absolute truths—statements that are objectively true for everyone. And, when it comes to the existence of God—whether there is a supreme, omnipotent Deity—either it's true for everyone or it's not true for anyone. The validity of God's existence has to be based on something other than just what we think. If you committed a crime, you'd never go into a courtroom and tell the judge that you don't believe he exists, or even that you don't believe he's a real judge. It wouldn't matter to him what you believe, he would still sentence you for your crime. Someday you, like all humanity, will stand before God (Hebrews 9:27). If you tell Him that you don't believe He exists, do you think He will cease to exist?

2) "YOU HAVE NO RIGHT TO TRY TO CONVERT ME TO YOUR BELIEFS."

This statement poses another self-contradicting thought. This person is telling you that you have no right to share your beliefs with him. However, by doing so, he is sharing his beliefs with you; and if what he said is true, then he has no right to do so. That reasoning should make someone think about the validity of this claim!

Everyone knows that in our country we *do* have the right to share our beliefs. This freedom of speech is guaranteed by the United States Constitution. The real question isn't about our *rights* to share our beliefs; it's really about whether or not those beliefs are based on truth.

3) "ALL RELIGIONS ARE BASICALLY THE SAME, SO CHOOSE WHICHEVER YOU LIKE."

Are all religions really the same? People who make this claim haven't done much homework on the beliefs of world religions. Religions such as Islam, Hinduism, Buddhism, Mormonism, and Christianity all teach widely varying views on essential doctrines: who (or what) God is, what the problem is in the world, how to solve it, what happens when we die, and so on. The religions have very different teachings, and since they make conflicting claims about reality, they can't all be true.

The simplest way to distinguish between Christianity and *all* other religions is this: In all manmade religions, man attempts to get right with God through a system of religious works—rituals, rules, traditions, good deeds, etc. Only in Christianity is it understood that man can never make himself right with God, and that God graciously offered His Son to make us right with Him. All other religions say *do*. Christianity says *done*. Done by Jesus Christ the Son of God, who, being without sin, took on our sins and died for us, thereby offering us the only provision that can make us right with God. Christ's death paid the penalty for our sins and if we repent and trust in Him alone, God will save us and give us eternal life. Acts 4:12 tells us, "Nor is there salvation in any other, for there is no other name under heaven given among men by which we must be saved."

Tullian Tchividjian, senior pastor at Coral Ridge Presbyterian Church in Ft. Lauderdale, Florida, says that Christians live their lives under a banner that says "It is Finished." He explains, "It's when you come to the heart realization that it is finished, when you come to the heart realization that Jesus plus nothing equals everything...then you're free. Jesus said, 'I have come to set the captives free.' So if you're a Christian, you're free...You're free because Jesus paid it all. It's finished, and that's good news." No other religion can offer that!

4) "YOU HAVE NO RIGHT TO IMPOSE YOUR MORALS ON ME."

When someone makes a statement like this, they've just done exactly what they said *you* couldn't do: they've imposed their morals on you, defining what you should or shouldn't do. Again, it's not a question of whether we have a *right* to make or share our moral judgments; we all make moral judgments throughout our day. It's a question of whether or not those moral judgments are based on truth. Now, we don't have the right to forcefully "impose" our morals on someone, but we most certainly do have the right to state what our morals are and why we believe in them. In fact, we are commanded by God to share our beliefs, and we are told to do so without quarreling and "in humility," while being "gentle to all, able to teach, patient" (2 Timothy 2:24,25). We are called to be "speaking the truth in love" (Ephesians 4:15).

A good way to diffuse this objection is to remind people that you are not making a moral judgment; you are just sharing with them what the Word of God says. You are basically telling them, "I didn't say it, God did." So, in essence, it's really about whether the Word of God is true. Jesus told us that His witness is true (John 8:14). So we need to stand firmly on the Word of God: the Bible says it; that settles it. I believe it!

5) "THE GOSPELS WERE WRITTEN BY MAN AND CAN'T BE TRUSTED."

As Christians we understand that the whole Bible is God's Word, given by inspiration of God (2 Timothy 3:16) and written down by man (as you would use a pen to write a letter). There is more manuscript evidence for the words of the Bible than for most ancient historical documents, and the latter are seldom called into question. Studying manuscript evidence and understanding how we got our Bible will greatly prepare you to answer this objection.

Another way to address the statement that the Bible cannot be trusted is to affirm the trustworthiness of Scripture using fulfilled prophecy. The Bible is unique among religious texts in that it contains hundreds of detailed prophecies, fulfilled with 100 percent accuracy. Since only an eternal, omniscient God knows the future, fulfilled prophecies can be very thought-provoking and convincing. There are over three hundred prophecies about Jesus alone. For example, the birth of Jesus was prophesied in great detail about seven hundred years before it occurred, and both biblical and secular historical documents verify that Jesus was born and lived into His early thirties. (Never accept a claim that Jesus didn't exist. That's absurd, and considering all the historical documentation of His life and ministry, no reputable scholar would make that claim. It's not likely you'll hear anyone deny the life of Jesus— but it has happened.)

The Bible is also filled with countless prophecies related to nations, leaders, and events. Another example of fulfilled prophecy involves the modern-day nation of Israel. The nation truly ceased to exist in A.D. 70, when the Roman army conquered Israel, destroying their temple and scattering the people throughout the known world. The prophet Daniel foretold of this destruction in Daniel 9:26, and there's much secular historical documentation to support these first-century events. Even Jesus spoke of the coming destruction of the Temple (Matthew 24:1,2; Luke 19:41–44; 21:5,6). The Scriptures also foretold that Israel would be regathered into its land and the nation would live again. After 1,878 years, on May 14, 1948, Israel became a nation in a day, just as the Bible prophesied (Isaiah 66:7,8; Jeremiah 16:14,15; Ezekiel 34:13; 37:10–14,21,22; Amos 9:14,15). No one can dispute that these prophecies have been fulfilled. They are historically well documented and are just two of hundreds of fulfilled prophecies that prove the Bible can be trusted as the inspired Word of God. The question then must be asked: If so many Bible prophecies have been fulfilled, why would anyone doubt the Bible? And, of the remaining prophecies that are yet to be fulfilled, why would anyone doubt that they would also be fulfilled? The Bible is self-proving and therefore is shown to be trustworthy. The real question is, "Why don't you trust it?"

6) "WHAT ABOUT PEOPLE WHO'VE NEVER HEARD OF JESUS CHRIST?"

God graciously reveals Himself to people throughout the world. Psalm 19:1–4 tells us, "The heavens declare the glory of God; and the firmament shows His handiwork. Day unto day utters speech, and night unto night reveals knowledge. There is no speech nor language where their voice is not heard. Their line has gone out through all the earth, and their words to the end of the world." Through what's known as general revelation, everyone, everywhere can look at creation and see that there must be a Creator. Even if they don't know Him, they should be thankful to Him. God reaches out to people, wherever they live, but people must respond. The question is, "What did you do with the knowledge that God has given you?"

God is good and just, and He will judge those who have not heard the gospel message based on their responses to what has been revealed to them. Do they see the sun, the moon, and the stars and know there is Someone who created them? All people, anywhere, should be able to know that. Or, do they choose some man to worship, or create a wooden object to worship? That's worshiping creation rather than the Creator. God will deal with primitive cultures that have never heard His name. In the meantime, we must care about those we know who have heard His name, who do have knowledge of Him and yet reject Him. Someday everyone will be held accountable for their answer to the question that Jesus asked Peter: "Who do you say that I am?" (Matthew 16:15).

> *God reaches out to people, wherever they live, but people must respond. The question is, "What did you do with the knowledge that God has given you?"*

7) "GANDHI DIDN'T BELIEVE IN JESUS, BUT HE MUST BE IN HEAVEN."

The world will often look at the good works of people like Gandhi and believe those works have saving power. Yet God says, "All our righteousnesses are like filthy rags" (Isaiah 64:6) and, "There is none who does good, no, not one" (Romans 3:12). Our works will never save us. Only Christ's work on the cross, paying the penalty for our sins, can save us. Jesus said, "I am the way, the truth, and the life. No one comes to the Father except through Me" (John 14:6). Only those who trust in Christ will go to heaven. We truly hope that Gandhi did trust in Christ before his death; however, there is no evidence that he did.

8) "JESUS WAS JUST A GOOD TEACHER...LIKE A LOT OF OTHER RELIGIOUS LEADERS."

Jesus did a lot of teaching during His earthly ministry and, yes, He was a good teacher. But unlike any other religious leader or teacher, Jesus claimed to be God. The claims that He made about His divinity offer only three options: 1) He was a liar (He claimed to be God, but He knew He wasn't); 2) He was a lunatic (He claimed to be God because He was crazy); or 3) He truly is who He says He is (He claimed to be God and He *is* God)! You choose. But unlike the founders of other religions, Jesus backed up His claims with countless miracles, proving He was God, then He rose from the dead, defeating death.

9) "YOU CAN'T PROVE THE RESURRECTION."

The accounts of Jesus' resurrection are supported by much historical evidence, from both biblical and secular documents. Yes, it's true you and I weren't there to personally see His resurrection, but many people were eyewitnesses and we have a written record of the events. He was seen by more than five hundred witnesses over a forty-day period, as He walked, and talked, and ate with His disciples and followers. And the resurrection took place after His death on the cross and His burial—three days after, just as the Scriptures and Jesus Himself repeatedly prophesied. Some skeptics will contend that our only real proof of the resurrection is historical accounts (they certainly don't accept biblical accounts). They say that because we weren't there, we can't prove it, so we can't believe it happened. This is not a legitimate objection. Since we can't go back in time to observe and verify *any* historical event, we readily rely on historical documents that detail when and how events occurred. This is really a question of whether the historical documents are accurate and trustworthy (we covered the authority of the Bible in #5).

Atheist Lee Strobel, a Yale Law School graduate, former award-winning legal editor of *The Chicago Tribune*, and a *New York Times* best-selling author, weighed the historical evidence he found in his nearly two-year investigation, and concluded the historical account of Jesus Christ to be true and supported by evidence inside and outside the Bible. Strobel was so convinced that he "took a step of faith in the same direction that the evidence was pointing" and repented of his sin and gave his life to Christ.[16]

Lastly, when talking with those who deny the resurrection, remember this: *If* the resurrection had not been true, it would have been easy for the people of that time to prove it false. All they had to do was produce the body. With the control of the Roman authority over the people and the power in numbers that they possessed, it would have been easy for them to find the body...*if* there had been one to find. As Christians, we *know* that we can believe the record of what the angels at the empty tomb proclaimed: "He is not here, but is risen! Remember how He spoke to you when He was still in Galilee, saying, 'The Son of Man must be delivered into the hands of sinful men, and be crucified, and the third day rise again'" (Luke 24:6,7).

10) "IT DOESN'T MATTER WHAT YOU BELIEVE, AS LONG AS YOU'RE SINCERE."

When it comes to your eternal destiny, it really *does* matter what you believe, and most importantly it matters in *whom* you put your faith and trust. People can be very sincere about something and still be wrong—sincerely wrong. The real question is whether or not you are putting your faith and trust in something that is *true*. Eternal life is available only to those who trust in Jesus Christ alone for their salvation, so being sincere about anything else is of no avail. Like with #1, you can believe gravity doesn't exist as you step out off a tenth-floor balcony. But no matter how sincere your belief, you will be *flat* wrong.

These are just ten of the many objections that skeptics will raise. The Bible tells us to "study to show thyself approved unto God, a workman that needeth not to be ashamed, rightly dividing the word of truth" (2 Timothy 2:15, KJV). It does take time to diligently study, but it is well worth the time and effort to be prepared to share your faith. Think of it this way: it is a privilege to preach the gospel and an honor that the God of the universe declares us worthy to do so. The apostle Paul reminds us, "How beautiful are the feet of those who preach the gospel of peace, who bring glad tidings of good things!" (Romans 10:15). In addition, discovering more answers for your own questions will also strengthen your faith and increase your trust in God.

IT'S ALL RELATIVE

Let's go back to #1 again and look a little more closely at relativism. It is likely the biggest problem emerging from today's post-modern way of thinking and is so widely embraced because it is "me"-centered. Everything is based upon what a person thinks and feels, not on any foundation of real truth.

Here's one way in which I've tried to diffuse this thinking and reason with people that there must be absolute truths. I've used the following illustration many times in my messages with very consistent responses.

I open with a simple question: "How tall am I?"

The students will readily start guessing: "Six feet," "Six foot four," and so on.

I respond by saying they are all wrong and I can't believe by how much. I then tell them that I am twelve feet tall! That elicits laughter, rolling of the eyes, and various comments: "Yeah, right." "No way!" "Where'd you go to school?," etc. I then pull out my trustworthy ruler that I have made, thereby assuring its accuracy. This ruler "proves" beyond a shadow of doubt that I am in fact twelve feet tall.

They still laugh and shake their heads, so I ask them why they don't believe me. They quickly inform me that my ruler is wrong, to which I promptly reply, "No, my ruler is perfect. I'm the teacher. I made it myself and I have verified its accuracy, so you can't tell me it's wrong!"

Of course I haven't changed their minds, so I then challenge them: "How can you prove me wrong?" Now it gets fun. They pull out a ruler and ask to compare it to mine, pointing out that the inches on their ruler are accurate and mine are different and therefore wrong. Then I say, "Well, that's your ruler, and it might be right for you, but this is my ruler and it's right for me. So you can't say that it's wrong just because you all think differently than I do. Should we vote on which ruler is correct? I'll get all my friends to vote with me and they'll tell you that my ruler is correct."

It's at this point that you can see the "lights" starting to come on for them. It's vitally important they understand that truth isn't based on a person's opinion or on a majority vote regardless of what our culture is telling us. Nor is it based on sincerity. I can sincerely believe my ruler is correct, but is it? There needs to be a verifiable, trustworthy standard, proven beyond a shadow of a doubt, to compare it to. In the case of measurements, such standards are defined by each country and are easily obtainable.

I then tell the students that if we want to know whether my ruler is accurate, it can't be determined based on my belief.

We have to take our rulers and compare them with the objective standard, and when we do we will see that their ruler is correct.

The point is that if we want to know if something is true, it doesn't matter what we *believe* about it, it matters whether there is accurate and trustworthy evidence to declare it to be true.

In #5 above, we've already shown the Word of God to be trustworthy and God to be faithful, by the detailed prophecies He's fulfilled. So, we can assuredly declare that the Bible is accurate and true and therefore must be deemed to be authoritative when setting the standards of morality, ethics, and faith. Despite the increase in moral relativism, we not only can confidently proclaim that God's Word is true from the very first verse, but we can use it to point people to the One who is Truth.

Tackling the Issue of "Race"

I firmly believe that all sixty-six books of the Bible are God's inspired Word and were written for our instruction. God tells us that (2 Timothy 3:16), and I believe it. The Bible helps us to address the "hot-button" issues of our culture, one of which is the problem of prejudice and tension between different so-called races. We in the church need to have biblical answers to this issue, as it is impacting the culture in a major way.

For example, many years ago, as I was preparing to marry Masami, I received a letter from my grandmother with the following words: "If you come to my house, I'll be the perfect hostess, but she [Masami] and I will never be friends!"

Masami and I were married in 1982, but I still remember the confusion I felt when I read that letter so many years ago. Why would my grandmother feel that way about someone she'd never met? Was it because Masami was a "bad" person? Was it because she was living an immoral life? No, that wasn't the case. Masami was a very kind and loving person. She actually worked in an orphanage, taking care of children who had been abandoned by their parents.

To be honest, if anyone should have received such a letter, it should have been Masami! I was the one who was living a totally immoral lifestyle. My precious wife-to-be should have received a letter saying, "You don't want to marry this guy. He's got a lot of issues." And it would have been the truth!

So why was it that my grandmother felt the way she did? Let me quote the next line of her letter: "Because your children will always have those eyes!"

To my grandmother, for me to marry a Japanese woman was just unacceptable. From her perspective, I was making a huge mistake. Not only was there a "racial" disparity, according to my grandmother, but those who had grown up in the WWII era harbored extremely negative feelings toward the Japanese in particular. My grandmother considered this an interracial marriage, and to her, that just wasn't right.

So what's the real deal with interracial marriage? Well, first, we need to get rid of the terms "races" and "interracial" altogether. Scientifically and biblically, there is only one race of people: *Homo sapiens*.

The major factor that most people use as a basis for racist attitudes is skin color. However, all humans actually have the same skin color. What we see on the outside is really just a matter of twelve genes and how they interact with the pigment (melanin) which we all have to some degree. The shade of skin is simply an external matter and has very little bearing on what truly makes the person.

Even secular scientists recognize that the main differences between people groups are really cultural, not genetic. Humans may have varied degrees of pigmentation, distinct physical characteristics, and different cultural habits, but according to our genetic makeup, we are essentially the same. In the famous human genome project, for example, scientists declared: "If you ask what percentage of your genes is reflected in your external appearance, the basis by which we talk about race, the answer seems to be in the range of .01 percent."[17] That tiny percentage is pretty insignificant.

Sadly, however, the influence of evolutionary teaching has caused untold damage to human relationships for centuries. Darwin's theory of evolution promotes the idea that people are divided into "advanced" and "primitive" races. The "more primitive" or "lower" races are supposedly most closely related to their ape-like ancestors; on the other side are the "advanced" races that are said to be superior to the rest. This has led to all sorts of racist attitudes, prejudice, hatred, division, and bloodshed.

Biblically, there is only one race of people: the human race. The Bible does talk about "peoples, tribes, tongues, and nations" (Revelation 11:9), but never races. That's because Acts 17:26 makes it very clear that we are all of "one blood" or one "race":

And He has made from one blood every nation of men to dwell on all the face of the earth, and has determined their preappointed times and the boundaries of their dwellings...

The Bible also makes it clear that all people are descendants of one man and one woman, Adam and Eve:

And so it is written, "*The first man Adam* became a living being." (1 Corinthians 15:45, emphasis added)

And the LORD God said, "It is *not good that man should be alone*; I will make him a helper comparable to him." (Genesis 2:18, emphasis added)

"And Adam called his wife's name Eve, because *she was the mother of all living.*" (Genesis 3:20, emphasis added)

In these verses, we see that there were no people before God created Adam, the first man. Adam was alone before God created the first woman, Eve; and Eve is the mother of all humans. All of humanity is related, made in the image of God. So we need to abandon the term "races" and instead talk about "cultures" or "people groups." If we were to do this, and follow the biblical perspective, it would greatly lessen the prejudice toward our fellow man.

Unfortunately, I wasn't raised believing this truth. When I was in high school, there was still a strong bias against the intermixing of blacks and whites. And to be honest, I have to say that I would never have considered marrying a black woman. That's just how I was raised. I am not proud of that fact.

The truth is, I was not any better than my grandmother on this issue. I had my own racist beliefs. In my high school, if a white girl dated a black guy, she was immediately ostracized. We wouldn't even talk to her anymore.

Please don't think I'm saying this is right. It's just how things were in Virginia at that time in my life. No one had ever taught me anything different on the topic, or had told me that all people are actually the same race.

After I moved to Lexington, Virginia, as a young teen, one of my first coaches was a black man named Coach Brown. He ran the Boys Club, where I practically lived. I was new in town, and with my own father gone from my life, I just didn't feel as if I fit in.

Coach Brown taught me how to play basketball, ping-pong, and the card game Hearts. He was a good man whom I greatly respect. He probably spent more time with me than my own father, and when I saw what an extraordinary person he was, I was forced to confront the racist feelings that I had. Inside, I knew something wasn't right about these negative feelings and attitudes. I just didn't know how to deal with them. It had always been easier for me to simply succumb to peer pressure and follow the crowd.

Sadly, I didn't have answers back then to deal with my grandmother's prejudice or even my own faulty thinking. I had to dig into God's Word for myself and read about the true origin of all people for me to get the answers I sought.

Racism, I believe, is actually a learned attitude; it's not a natural instinct. One day while working as a camp counselor in Jamaica I was sitting and talking with some young children at the camp. One of my team members, Nate, was walking up the path with one of the young girls attending the camp, and was holding her hand as they walked. There were two young Jamaican girls, about nine years old, sitting next to me and I overheard their conversation. One young lady said to her friend, "Look at the girl there with that boy, mon. Do you think he's her brother?" (I can't begin to write in the beautiful Jamaican accent!)

You've got to understand, Nate was red-headed, freckled, and as "white" as you can get. The girl walking with him had very dark skin.

The other young lady looked at her friend and said, "No, mon, he's not her brother. Can't you see, she's black and he's white?"

It struck me that day that seeing these external, superficial differences has to be taught. It is a learned and conditioned response. The one young lady was just seeing a young man walking with a child, and because of the caring gesture of holding her hand, thought he might be her brother. The other young lady had learned to observe a "difference" in them based solely on skin color.

That is why I take such a strong stand on this issue today. I know I was wrong in my racist attitudes when I was young, and there is no doubt in my mind that there are thousands of people who believe the same way I did at that time in my life. So when I have the opportunity to share what God's Word says on this topic, I don't hesitate. We have to teach people the truth about racism, but what bothers me the most is that the church has dropped the ball on this issue. In fact, the church (in some instances) is one of the last bastions of racism and prejudice in America. And if we, as Christians, cannot grasp the need to eradicate racism, how can we expect the world to do that?

DOES RACE MATTER?

I know from the responses of pastors and church members where I speak that some in the church are failing to take the high road on this issue. When I begin talking to people about the biblical answer to racism, I always ask a multiple-choice question to see where the audience is on this topic. Here's the question:

How many different "races" are there in the world?

a) 1

b) 6

c) 8

d) More than 10

e) It doesn't matter!

I almost always get the same answer from the church: e) It doesn't matter!

It's nice that people desire to be "color-blind" when it comes to relating to people who have a different color skin than their own. But friends, if you've grown up with a background like mine, it really does matter. What we believe about race greatly influences our spiritual walk and our interactions with other people. To illustrate how much it matters, let me share just a few examples of experiences I've had since starting in full-time, vocational ministry.

- One time in North Carolina, after I spoke, a man came up to me and shared about one of his close friends. His friend was a deacon in his church, and his job was to approach anyone with a different "skin tone" who happened to visit the church and tell them which church they may be "more comfortable in" next week. (Can you believe that?)

- After I gave a seminar in Indianapolis, Indiana, two black ladies shared with me how they had harbored attitudes of racism themselves as a consequence of their upbringing. One of the women confessed to me that she had dissuaded her son from dating a certain young lady because she was "too black"! This mom had equated darker skin with primitiveness. After she heard me speak, she regretted her attitudes and actions.

- Recently, I was scheduled to speak at a church in Tennessee. However, when the pastor learned that my wife was Japanese, he canceled the event because of my so-called interracial marriage. His church's bylaws state that if he lets a man speak who is in an "interracial" marriage, the pastor would be removed from ministry.

- In Kentucky, one pastor asked me upon my arrival not to give the "race" talk because he had invited the congregation down the street and they didn't allow "black people" to join their church. (Remember, there are no "black" people or "white" people; we're all some shade of brown!) After I spoke with the host pastor about the content of the talk, he asked that I just remove the "interracial marriage" part. I prayed that night about that approach, but the next day I told him I just couldn't do that in good conscience. If I was going to give the talk, I had to present it as it had been prepared. I couldn't start pulling out parts for fear that someone may be offended. He agreed that I could give the talk as I normally do. At the end of the talk this pastor stood up in front of the audience and fully endorsed the message. I applaud his ability to overcome his apprehension and take a courageous stance in his church and community.

Once I became a Christian and began studying the Bible, I came to a better understanding of where such prejudice can come from. In Scripture, God often tells His people not to intermarry with those from pagan cultures, but it is always for spiritual reasons and not because of skin color or "race." God called the Israelites to be a holy people, set apart for Him. He commanded that they love Him with all their heart, soul, and strength and that they worship Him only, and that meant not intermingling with pagan cultures that worshiped false gods. It had nothing to do with skin color.

WHERE DO "RACES" COME FROM?

I can't tell you the number of times I've been approached and asked about a variety of teachings on where black people came from. It's been suggested to me that black people are the result of the mark on Cain, or the curse of Ham (neither of those ideas is scriptural). I've even had people present a theory that humans actually mated with apes to create black people. (I wish I were joking about that one, but I'm not. And sadly more than one person has asked me if it's true.)

In Utah, I spoke with a Mormon man who shared with me what his religion taught him. He believes there are different colored folks on earth because of their actions while in "pre-existence." According to Mormon theology, prior to receiving a human body, each person had a spirit body. Mormons believe Jesus and Lucifer were spirit brothers, and each brought a plan to their father, God (of course, this is not the true God!), regarding how these spirits who would receive a human body should be "saved." God preferred Jesus' plan, so Lucifer (hereafter known as Satan) got upset and caused a rebellion. There was a war, with many of the spirits taking sides in the battle. Those who fought on Jesus' side received a body with blond hair and blue eyes. You guessed it: those who fought on Satan's side got black skin. And, in case you were wondering, those who stayed neutral and didn't take a side received "middlebrown" skin with their human body. This belief, of course, is totally unbiblical. We could easily laugh at this one, if it weren't so sad that the Mormon church teaches such lies.

Ultimately, the issue of racism comes down to this: where did humans come from? We have to answer this question in order to understand "race." What people believe about our origins makes a tremendous difference.

In reflecting on what I was taught in America's secular educational system (where my grandmother was also educated), I now realize that our beliefs about "races" were greatly influenced by erroneous teachings in the schools. When you reject what the Bible teaches about the origin of man—that all people came from Adam and Eve (Genesis 1:22; 3:20)—you will end up with all kinds of wrong beliefs. The reality is that many Christians have rejected biblical history on this issue.

It was here, in the "public" schools, that I was taught it was a *fact* that humans evolved over millions of years. It was here that I was taught it was a *fact* that there are different "races" of people, and that some "races" were "better" than others.

When you realize how widespread racism and evolutionary teaching were in America, then you can understand why many people from my grandmother's generation believed the way they did. The following text, from a 1920s middle school textbook, is a sample of the teachings from that period:

> Mankind is divided into five races. The yellow and white races are extremely strong and diligent. Because the other

races are feeble and stupid, they are going to be extermi-
nated by the white race. Only the yellow race competes
with that race. This is so-called evolution.[18]

The reality is this: *If* evolution were true, and *if* man really
did evolve from a common ape-like ancestor over millions of
years, then the racists are right: some "races" really are more
advanced than others. And *if* that were true, then it would be
understandable why people like my grandmother and my
friends in high school held onto their wrong beliefs.

But let me be clear here: I'm not blaming evolution for
racism! Racism has been around long before Charles Darwin
popularized his theories about the potential mechanism for
evolution. Because society generally adopted evolution as a
fact, though, there were consequences. Consider what well-
known scientist Stephen Gould, a non-Christian and anti-
creationist, had to say about Darwin's impact:

> Biological arguments for racism may have been com-
> mon before 1850, but they increased by orders of mag-
> nitude following the acceptance of evolutionary theory.[19]

Many people are familiar with Charles Darwin's book *On
the Origin of Species*, written in 1859. But how many of us
know the original title of his book? When I speak, I've found
that most people aren't aware of the original title: *On the
Origin of Species by Means of Natural Selection, or the Preser-
vation of Favoured Races in the Struggle for Life.*

Now you understand why the title was shortened! In our
politically correct culture, it doesn't sound good to talk about
"favoured races." According to evolutionary theory, some
"races" are more "favoured" than others. Whites are supposedly at the top of the heap, with blacks at the bottom, closer to
the "missing ape-like ancestor link." It's easy to see how this
belief about the origin of "races" helps to fuel bigotry.

IS RACISM GENETIC?

One of the consequences of adopting this belief system is ethnic cleansing. In his BreakPoint column, Chuck Colson writes about the cause of ethnic cleansing in Bosnia, according to an article in the *Boston Globe* (not exactly a bastion of conservatism):

> The cause of the bloodbath in Bosnia, says the *Globe*, lies in our genes...
>
> "Xenophobia [fear of foreigners] has apparently arisen in the course of natural selection and social evolution," [anthropologist Charles] Southwick writes.
>
> It's an evolutionary "adaptation" just like the tiger's claws or eagle's feathers.[20]

Here is how this supposedly works. Millions of years ago, when we were "hominids" living in a primitive environment, just enough resources would have existed for our group to survive. If another group of hominids moved into our environment, there were big problems. There wouldn't be enough resources for both groups to survive. Well, some of the hominids had a gene that led them to be more aggressive, and they would kill off the hominids in the other group. This would result in that gene being passed on to the next generation. So, you see, hating those who look different from us is "genetic"! It's not our fault!

Based on a 2005 study by Arizona State University researchers, *ScienceDaily* reports:

> Contrary to what most people believe, the tendency to be prejudiced is a form of common sense, hard-wired into the human brain through evolution as an adaptive response to protect our prehistoric ancestors from danger.[21]

In reality, though, we don't see this attitude occurring naturally in kids. As I mentioned earlier, I believe racism has to be taught. Have you noticed that children can be perfectly comfortable growing up around others from all kinds of different "races," cultures, ethnicities, and languages and not harbor racist attitudes at all? Friends, if hating someone because of skin tone, eye shape, or hair texture is genetic, there's nothing we can do about it. But if hating someone for those reasons is sin, there is something we can do about it. It's called *repent!*

People need to stop making minor differences like skin shade and eye shape a big deal, and do what God does: He doesn't look at the outside appearance (1 Samuel 16:7), but the inside—a person's heart. And He sees all of us as descendants of Adam, all members of the one human race.

When we start viewing people the way God tells us to—by not looking at the outward appearance—we will recognize that every person on this planet, regardless of external appearance, is beautiful and valuable to God. Every person is a sinner in need of a Savior, whose name is Jesus Christ. Genesis is not full of fairy tales. It is real history, and that history helps solve the racism problem.

By the way, what we see in the world around us supports the fact that we all descend from one man and one woman as the Bible teaches. For example, mitochondrial DNA, which is passed from the mother to the offspring, shows that every person on this planet descended from one woman.[22] The Y-chromosome, which is passed from the father to the child, shows that every person on this planet descended from one man.[23] A *lot* of time and money could have been saved on that research if they had only believed what God said! His Word tells us plainly, "In the beginning *God created...*" (Genesis 1:1).

The Bitter Fruit of Evolution

A s we have seen, beliefs have consequences. History is marred with examples of the horrors that can happen when people believe certain "races" are superior to others. Consider the Australian Aborigines. Scientists classified them as the closest living relative to the "missing link," or believed they might even be the "missing link." The Australian Museum in Sydney actually published a booklet listing Aborigines under the designation of "Australian animals." The same booklet included instructions on how to rob graves to obtain specimens, as well as how to plug bullet holes in the freshly killed individuals.[24]

The government accepted that classification and it impacted the way the Aboriginals were treated. They were hunted like animals. They were skinned and their skins stuffed and put on display in museums. Many of the women were "forcibly bred" by white men. (Let's call it what it really was: rape.) This was done to supposedly breed the "blackness" or "primitiveness" out of the next generation of children.

While I spoke recently in the U.K., there was a battle going on in the court system. The Aboriginal descendants were fighting to have the bones of their ancestors returned to them from the London Natural History Museum so they could be given a proper burial. Some scientists opposed sending the bones back for a very interesting reason. Let me quote from an article in 2003 by Nicholas Glass:

> Aborigines from Australia and Tasmania have been asking for the bones of their ancestors to be returned for burial. But scientists here are concerned that if these bones go back, their value for scientific research will be lost forever.[25]

If we read between the lines, we see that the "value for scientific research" means that scientists believe the bones help "prove" that these people were more closely related to apes.

It's not just in Australia that these types of events have occurred. Here in America, the new science of anthropology was put on display at the 1904 World's Fair in St. Louis. The man responsible for the exhibits had one ambition: to show the superiority of the "white race."

St. Louis was also hosting the 1904 Summer Olympics. To coincide with the real Olympics taking place, W. J. McGee and James Sullivan organized an "ethnic Olympics" they called Anthropology Days. Its purpose was to show how inferior the "savages" were compared with "civilized man," but let's call it what it really was: racism.

THE TRAGIC PRACTICE OF EUGENICS

Another result of evolutionary thinking is the practice of eugenics. According to biologist George William Hunter (whose controversial textbook, *Civic Biology*, was at the heart of the Scopes trial), eugenics is "the science of being well born."

Interesting! The term *eugenics* actually comes from the Greek roots for "good" and "generation" or "origin," and was first used to refer to "the science of heredity" around 1883. Simply put, eugenics is the study of hereditary improvement of the human race by controlled selective breeding.

In the early 1900s, nationwide contests took place where awards were given to families that supposedly had the "best breeding." At fairs and exhibitions, eugenicists hosted "fitter family" and "better baby" competitions. The winner, like a prize steer, was awarded a medal or a blue ribbon.

So what was the goal of eugenicists? People actually believed they were making society better. If there really are "favoured races" as Darwin proposed, then some "races" are more advanced than others. If only the "best" were allowed to procreate, that would make future generations even better, and over time this would help the human species to continue to evolve into a superior race. Consider these quotes:

> The goal was to immediately sterilize fourteen million people...and millions more worldwide—the "lower tenth"—and then continuously eradicate the remaining lowest tenth until only a pure Nordic super race remained.[26]

> Leaders of the ophthalmology profession conducted a long and chilling political campaign to round up and coercively sterilize every... [person] with a vision problem.[27]

Ouch! Let me illustrate this for you. If you are reading this wearing glasses or contacts, or you've had Lasik surgery, or you have any vision problems at all, it would have been: Snip! Snip! No kids for you!

Nationwide, at least 60,000 people were coercively sterilized at that time. What does that mean? Again, let me illustrate. If you were considered to be the wrong race, lower class, or "feebleminded," you could be thrown in jail until you were beyond the age of breeding unless you "voluntarily" agreed to be sterilized. If you agreed to be sterilized, you could remain free.

In my seminars, when I ask people where they think these horrible practices occurred, most say they believe this happened in Nazi Germany. However, all of this took place in *America* years before the Third Reich rose to power in Germany. In fact, Adolf Hitler actually borrowed much of the "scientific" research and many of the philosophies and practices of the United States and implemented them in Germany.

What a tragic impact belief in evolution has had on this culture! Yes, in the "home of the free," it was actually legal for the U.S. government to forcibly sterilize or even kill those considered unsuitable for reproducing:

> One hundred years ago, Indiana became the first place in the world to allow state authorities to sterilize anyone considered unfit for procreation, a practice known as eugenics.[28]

In 1907, Indiana Governor Frank Hanley signed into effect the Compulsory Sterilization Law, mandating the sterilization of criminals and "mental defectives." Indiana started by sterilizing men in prisons before the law was passed. (By the way, these men weren't given any painkiller for the procedure.)

I attended high school in Virginia, and my senior year was 1979. In Virginia alone, between 1924 and 1979, about 8,000 citizens were sterilized for eugenic reasons. They were still sterilizing people when I was in school there and I had no idea.

It was also against the law in sixteen states for a person of "color" to marry a "white" person. The laws prohibiting "interracial" marriage were called "miscegenation laws." It took a ruling from the Supreme Court, *Loving v. Virginia*, to strike these laws down in 1967.

EMBRACING FALSE TEACHING

Let me ask you a question: in the 1930s through 1960s, was America more or less "Christian" than it is today?

Let me help you with this: during that time frame, could you walk into the secular schools and see a Bible on the teacher's desk? Could he or she read from it? Could a teacher pray aloud in school? Could you walk into a business and say "Merry Christmas" and not feel like you were breaking the law? The answer to all of these is, of course, yes!

How could this "Christian" nation pass the unbiblical laws that we have passed? Take a look at this quote:

> *We, the body of Christ, passed these laws because we bought into the false history of evolution. With our lips we said "Jesus," but with our lives, we lived "Darwin"!*

> One reason the religious eugenics movement was so large was because "evangelical scholars were among the first to embrace Darwin's theory of evolution, and did so well in advance of its widespread acceptance by the scientific community."[29]

The reason we could pass such laws then is the same reason churches today can cancel my speaking engagements because I'm in what they believe to be an "interracial" marriage. People in our nation now believe that the Bible is not authoritative, and they act as if "freedom of religion" is "freedom *from* religion," which it is not. In the schools, kids are being taught that there are different "races" and that some are "preferable" or more advanced than others.

We, the body of Christ, passed these laws because we bought into the false history of evolution. This shows that there are consequences to beliefs. With our lips we said "Jesus," but with our lives, we lived "Darwin"!

If we had stood firm on the truth of biblical history, this "Christian" nation would not have passed the laws we did or treated humans the way we've treated them. We know that God does not condone practices like racism, eugenics, and forced sterilization because the Word of God is clear on such things. We must approach these topics with boldness and confidence, starting with the Word as our foundation. As Christians, we need to begin studying the Bible so we have biblical responses to issues like these. If we don't learn from the mistakes we have made in the past, we are destined to repeat them again in the future.

Paul warned the early church about accepting falsehood as truth. He wrote, "For the time will come when they will not endure sound doctrine, but according to their own desires, because they have itching ears, they will heap up for themselves teachers; and they will turn their ears away from the truth, and be turned aside to fables" (2 Timothy 4:3,4). Christians have sinned by accepting and embracing false and unbiblical teachings when we should be soundly rejecting them.

We have swallowed fables and false teaching in the past when we accepted man's wisdom over God's Word. Unfortunately, based on what I've discovered in my travels, many are still doing it today. The fact that all humans are of one race biologically is clearly taught in the Bible. God created man and woman as one race. When the families were scattered across the earth at the time of the Tower of Babel, they each took different combinations of genes with them. In such small populations, trivial differences (such as skin color) can arise quickly in only a few generations. That is why different people groups speak different languages and have slightly different genetic traits. But there's no room for anyone to say that some people groups are more "advanced" than others. We're all close relatives who share the same ancestors and the same blood line— and all of us can be saved by the blood of the same Savior, Jesus Christ.

A SENSE OF HOPELESSNESS

Evolutionary theory has had another consequence in the U.S. and around the world, impacting not only how we view others but also how we view ourselves.

The research that I've seen suggests that as many as 70 percent of high school students will contemplate committing suicide at some in their schooling.[30] Researchers often don't understand why there is a sense of purposelessness and hopelessness among so many public school students.

Suicide is one of the leading causes of teenage death in the world today. In Australia and Japan, countries where I have a number of friends, *suicide has become the number one cause of teenage death*. In America, suicide is the third highest cause of death among teenagers today![31]

Why is this happening? Simple: kids have no sense of value or purpose. That's what happens when you take generations of young people and teach them that they came from slime. They have no clue why they are here on earth. They have no idea where they're going. Their teachers in the public schools convince them that they just evolved by chance, and they are simply more advanced animals with no intrinsic value. If that's true, then when life is tough, why not end it all? After all, there is absolutely no purpose or meaning in life. And when you die, there is nothing.

My friends, that is a lie from the pit of hell! This false line of thinking breaks my heart, and it breaks God's heart, too. Psalm 139 says:

> For You formed my inward parts;
>> You covered me in my mother's womb.
> I will praise You, for I am fearfully and wonderfully made;
>> Marvelous are Your works,
>> And that my soul knows very well.
> My frame was not hidden from You,
>> When I was made in secret,
>> And skillfully wrought in the lowest parts of the earth.
> Your eyes saw my substance, being yet unformed.
>> And in Your book they all were written,
>> The days fashioned for me,
>> When as yet there were none of them.
> (Psalm 139:13–16)

I'm sure you can see how much damage the theory of evolution has done to the Christian faith, and how these teachings have eroded the biblical foundation of our great nation. We are reaping its bitter fruit, especially among our youth. How can we change the attitudes of kids in this generation? How can we make them realize that each of them is uniquely created in the image of God and that He loves them? It's up to us to share the truth with others, explaining to them that God created all people, according to Genesis chapter 1—all are equally valuable—and that He has a plan and a purpose for every single life. Only by helping people understand the true history of mankind can we point them to the only true hope for the future.

Seeing the Grand Design

G od had a plan from the very beginning and we see His beautiful plan of redemption woven throughout the Bible—a scarlet thread, the blood of Jesus, that stretches from the Garden to eternity. God tells us that without the shedding of blood there is no forgiveness of sin (Leviticus 17:11; Hebrews 9:22). The Bible gives many wonderful pictures that point to how Christ redeems us. One of those is Christ as our Kinsman Redeemer. Two beautiful examples of this are the redemption of slaves as provided for in the Mosaic Law, and the Law of Levirate Marriage.

First, redemption of a slave. The Bible tells us in Leviticus 25:47–55 that when a poor Israelite sold himself into slavery to a foreigner (a non-Israelite), he could be redeemed by one of his kin prior to the year of Jubilee (the time when the law required the emancipation of slaves).

God provided for our redemption from slavery to sin, by our near Kinsman, Jesus Christ, and we now serve Him, as 1 Corinthians 7:23 tells us: "You were bought at a price; do not become slaves of men."

Another beautiful biblical picture of redemption is that of the kinsman redeemer depicted in the book of Ruth. This short book of the Bible beautifully showcases God's provision in the Law of Levirate Marriage, and it points to Jesus Christ. (Levirate comes from the Latin word *levir*, meaning "husband's brother.")

By Mosaic law a man was obligated to marry his brother's widow if she was childless (Deuteronomy 25:5; Matthew 22:25). If a younger brother was unable or unwilling to do so, the next of kin would step forward to marry the widow. This law was put in place to perpetuate the brother's family name and preserve his property within the tribe. The nearest kinsman would first pay the price, redeem any debt the widow had, then he would marry her. The book of Ruth is a beautiful love story of a widow redeemed by her nearest of kin. The kinsman redeemer, as pictured here, foreshadows our Kinsman Redeemer, Jesus Christ. For those who come to Him in humble repentance and trust, Christ redeems our debt (sin) by paying the price with His blood and then we become His bride.

In both cases, slavery and widowhood, where redemption was accomplished by a kinsman redeemer, there were several requirements.

1. The kinsman redeemer must be a blood relative, a member of the family. In Jesus, God became a man, flesh and blood. He is God, but as our Kinsman Redeemer He came in human form.

    And the Word became flesh and dwelt among us, and we beheld His glory, the glory as of the only begotten of the Father, full of grace and truth. (John 1:14)

    For both He who sanctifies [Christ] and those who are being sanctified are all of one, for which reason He is not ashamed to call them brethren. (Hebrews 2:11)

2. The kinsman redeemer must be able to pay the price. He must have the necessary means to be able to redeem the property or the person. Jesus was able to redeem us because He paid the price with His own pure blood.

   ...knowing that you were not redeemed with corruptible things, like silver or gold, from your aimless conduct received by tradition from your fathers, but with the precious blood of Christ, as of a lamb without blemish and without spot. (1 Peter 1:18,19)

3. The kinsman redeemer must be willing to redeem. The Law allowed for a kinsman to refuse to redeem (Deuteronomy 25:7). We see this in Ruth 4:6, where Ruth's closest kin was unwilling, so Boaz, as the next of kin, stepped forward to redeem her. He was willing to redeem both Ruth's debt (the land of her deceased husband) and Ruth (in marriage). Jesus was not only *able* to redeem us by paying the price with His blood, He was also *willing* to do so. He willingly gave up His own life:

   "For even the Son of Man did not come to be served, but to serve, and to give His life a ransom for many." (Mark 10:45)

   ...our great God and Savior Jesus Christ, who gave Himself for us, that He might redeem us from every lawless deed and purify for Himself His own special people, zealous for good works. (Titus 2:13,14)

We are slaves to sin, and we have a debt we can never pay; we are dead in our trespasses and sin (John 8:34). We need a kinsman who is *able* and *willing* to pay the price. Jesus is that Kinsman Redeemer for all who come to Him in faith! God's plan was there from the very beginning and He is gracious in giving us such clear and beautiful pictures so that we might understand—how precious is the blood of Jesus. Go tell others about Him.

PREACHING FROM THE GRAVE

I've always been inspired by the story of the British preacher and author John Bunyan, maybe because I feel a kinship with him. Like me, Bunyan was a product of a humble background and had very little formal schooling. Yet God empowered him to have great influence through his spiritual writings.

It may be hard to believe, but John Bunyan has been preaching from his grave since his death in 1688. Let me share with you a bit of his remarkable story.

At the age of thirty, John Bunyan was arrested and imprisoned for preaching without a license (a requirement of the Church of England, the state church). From his cell, Bunyan began writing his now-famous book, *The Pilgrim's Progress* (full title: *The Pilgrim's Progress—From This World to That Which Is to Come; Delivered under the Similitude of a Dream*). It's reported to be the second best-selling book of all time, surpassed only by the Bible. Bunyan also penned a book that may be the most-read English autobiography of all time: *Grace Abounding to the Chief of Sinners.*

Considered a heretic and a Nonconformist by the established Church of England during his day, Bunyan was not allowed to be buried in the usual church graveyards. As with the other Nonconformists, his body had to be laid to rest elsewhere.

Today, Bunyan's tomb in London has become a highly visited place. It just so happens to stand opposite the chapel of the famous evangelist John Wesley.

On each side of Bunyan's tomb, visitors can see sculptures summarizing the message of *The Pilgrim's Progress*. One sculpture shows the book's main character, Pilgrim, with a burden

John Bunyan's tomb

on his back. The other shows Pilgrim kneeling before the cross of Christ with the burden falling off his back. This is really a simple depiction of the gospel message of Christ—and it's being preached every day right at John Bunyan's tomb!

By the way, just as you would expect from someone who was unwilling to compromise with the "authorities" of his time, Bunyan believed in six literal days of creation. He wrote about the first ten chapters of the book of Genesis as being real history.

John Bunyan's autobiography opens with his wonderful testimony. Bunyan, explaining why he wrote about his life, said he discovered in God's Word that Christians have an obligation to share their story of how God has worked in their lives. It's not something we should do for ourselves or to impress family and friends. It's to be done as a service to remind other believers of God's goodness and as a testimony to the world (nonbelievers).

Bunyan wrote, "Wherefore this I have endeavoured to do; and not only so, but to publish it also; that, if God will, others may be put in remembrance of what he hath done for their souls, by reading his work upon me."[32]

In essence, Bunyan is saying that the Lord would want us (as He did the children of Israel in Joshua 4) to set up stones, or memorials, to remember what He has done in our lives. I believe we have a duty not only to tell the next generation about God's deliverance, but also to share with our children about God's provision in the toughest and most terrifying moments of our lives. We should be open to sharing with them how God corrected us in our sins and showed His goodness toward us even in the consequences of those sins. Our lives, in all things—both good times and bad—should be a testimony to Him.

Remember, you don't have to be a brilliant thinker to minister to others and answer their questions about the Bible. The Lord is looking for obedience from us, not necessarily an advanced degree. Maybe you've heard this before: God doesn't call the qualified, He qualifies the called.

SHARING FAITH, HOPE, AND LOVE

One opportunity I had to minister to others was when our ministry had the privilege of hosting over two hundred people on an Alaskan cruise. One of the first things I do on a cruise ship is locate some of the ship's staff members who are Christians. I always try to encourage them, as I know they work in a tough environment. They're away from their families—and many times away from their home countries—and that can be a challenge.

On this particular cruise, I met a Christian man from Indonesia. I told him that I'd love to come and fellowship with him and the other Christians if possible. He was so excited and told me they were having a meeting the next night. They had to get together at 2 a.m. because these folks worked very long shifts and that was their only free time.

To meet the Christian staff early that next morning, I brought along some of the members from our ministry. As we walked through the crew area, we could hear dance music pounding through the speakers and could tell there was a happenin' party going on down the hall. When we got to the "party room," we stopped. I'll never forget that moment: there we were, standing in the hallway between two doors. We were at a crossroads. If we walked through the door to our left, we'd be in with those partying. Disco lights flashed as the music thumped and people milled about dancing, drinking, and having a great time. To be honest, it looked like they were having lots of fun.

Our other choice was to go through the doorway to our right and be with the Christians. It was a small, quiet room with only about five people in it and nothing very fancy to make it look enticing. To be honest, it really did not look like tons of fun. But we went in and joined this small group of brothers and sisters from around the globe. They didn't have a cool stereo system. No booze. No dancing. All they had was an old, beat-up guitar with only three strings. But as we started to sing songs of praise to the Lord, it was one of the most beautiful sounds I've ever heard.

The room filled with the voices of people singing praises to the Lord, each in his or her own language. I could hear people singing in at least four different languages. I couldn't understand all their words, but I knew the song by heart: "The Old Rugged Cross." The memory of the fellowship we shared that night will remain with me forever.

Every day, you and I walk down this path of life and come to critical points along the way. We reach crossroads where we have to decide which way we are going to turn. Most of the time, the room to the left looks like "the place to be." It promises immediate gratification and pleasure. Usually, it looks like a lot more fun. But Proverbs 14:12 says, "There is a way that seems right to a man, but its end is the way of death."

That night on the ship, as we worshiped together, we didn't have massive numbers of people. The singing, especially mine, didn't sound that great when compared to the high-tech music blasting across the hall. To Jesus, though, it was a beautiful sound.

Those crew members were so encouraged by our willingness to spend time in praise and worship with them that night. Before we left, they gave us big hugs and told us that no one had ever joined them in their meeting before. Yes, we need to be out sharing our faith with the lost and telling them the reasons for our hope. But we also need to remember to fellowship and minister to Christians and "love on the living," as well!

Please allow me to challenge you to make sure your life truly reflects God's priorities. Rather than choosing fleeting pleasures, we should be keenly aware of opportunities to give encouragement and hope to people. When we invest in people's lives, we honor the Lord.

SHARING MY STORY

One time, while I was in Louisiana, I was asked if I'd go speak to children who were classified as "wards of the state." I said, "Sure!" without even thinking. Frankly, I was shocked as we drove up to what looked like a prison and were required to sign in. I was told that these children had not necessarily done anything wrong; they just didn't have any family to take care of them, so the state had to provide for them. These children were being raised in what was essentially a jail. Wow! And I had thought my teenage years were rough.

For the presentation, we were led into a large Day Room that would hold about a hundred and fifty people. After setting up my projector and getting the computer working, I sat down and talked with my friend as we waited for the youth to come in. About ten minutes later, in walked seven teenage girls. That was it! Now, please don't take this the wrong way, but if I had known my audience was going to be seven teenage girls, I probably wouldn't have agreed to come. Not because of the number; I really don't care about that. As I've said before, my job isn't to worry about how many folks are in the audience, it's to deliver the message that God has placed on my heart in a way that points people to Jesus and His Word.

Honestly, I just felt uncomfortable because I don't consider myself the type of person who can really minister to teenage girls. Guys are a different story; I can relate to guys because I am one. In addition, I knew that I couldn't do a formal presentation for only seven people; it seems hokey. So my presentation was out the window, too. That made me very nervous. Without my presentation notes and visuals as my outline to keep me on track, my mind runs all over the place. I've often joked about having ADD (Attention Deficit Disorder), but it's the truth. I can quickly get out of focus.

Suddenly, I remembered the wise words that my friend Mark Cahill had told me long before. "Carl," he had said, "evangelism is a conversation, not a presentation!" (Look up the word "conversation" in an 1828 Webster's Dictionary sometime; you may be surprised by its definition.) So I decided that rather than giving these teens a presentation, we'd just converse!

I told the young ladies who I was and where I was from, and I shared with them the types of issues I have dealt with in my life. I then asked if they had any questions or if there was anything they were dealing with in which I could encourage them. These young ladies immediately started asking lots of in-depth questions. That's not common! Usually, getting teenagers to talk and ask questions is a battle, but not with these young ladies. They just jumped right in, asking really good questions.

I noticed one young lady sitting quietly who didn't seem to be at all "on board" with the conversation. In fact, I could have seen the chip on her shoulder from the next state! She didn't want to be there; that fact came through loud and clear. After I had answered the other girls' questions for about thirty minutes, this young lady finally raised her hand. *Cool!* I thought to myself. *She's coming around.*

"Yes, ma'am," I said to her.

She asked, "Do you believe that God knows every baby that comes to this planet?"

"Yes, I do!" I replied without hesitation.

She then looked me in the eyes and asked, "Then why would God allow a thirteen-year-old girl to get raped, get pregnant, and have a baby?" Ouch! That's as "real world" as it gets.

I just knew in my heart that she was talking about herself. It's at moments like this when all the philosophical and theological training you've ever had goes out the window. Waxing eloquent on the character of God, using pious words that no one understands, was not going to help me connect with this hurting teenage girl.

But it's amazing how God works. I'd been preparing a talk using 2 Corinthians 12:9,10 and Romans 5:3,4. I'd been reading those verses and was struggling with them, quite frankly. The passage in 2 Corinthians tells us that God's strength is made perfect in weakness. With my background, I didn't understand that at all. With a father who was a professional wrestler, I just couldn't show weakness. As an air-traffic controller, I most definitely couldn't show weakness; the guys I worked with would tear me apart the moment they found a vulnerable spot.

It got worse, though. This passage also says that we're to "take pleasure in infirmities." That word "infirmities" means "troubles, difficulties, and challenges." God is telling us to take pleasure in troubles, difficulties, and challenges? How is that possible? I felt that, all too often, we not only do not take pleasure in distresses, but rather we argue and fight about silly things, like the carpet color in the sanctuary. But right at that moment, when this girl asked her question, the Holy Spirit tore the blinders off of my eyes and illuminated those verses for me.

I opened my Bible and read the following verse to the girl:

> And He [Jesus] said to me, "My grace is sufficient for you, for My strength is made perfect in weakness." Therefore most gladly I will rather boast in my infirmities, that the power of Christ may rest upon me. (2 Corinthians 12:9)

I told her, "You know, I've really struggled with the meaning of that verse until right now. I think I finally understand what God is talking about here." I paused. And when I opened my mouth again, I started to share information about myself that I had kept private for much too long. "I've never talked about this with anyone," I began, "but I was sexually abused by two uncles growing up. So I understand what you're feeling. You are at a crossroads in your life. One choice you have is to allow what happened in your past circumstances to determine your value, but that will lead you down a very ugly road. Trust me; I lived that life until I was twenty-six years old, and it was not pretty." (It wasn't until I became a Christian that I made a different choice.)

"You also have another option," I continued. "It is to choose to allow what God has done for you to determine your value. And the fact is that Jesus loves you so much that while you were still spitting on Him and driving the nails into His wrists and feet (which is what our sin did), He chose to die for you, to pay for your sins, so you can have an eternal life in relationship with Him. We live in a world that lies to us; it tells us that what we have, what we look like, or what we do determines our value. But if our value is based on anything that we bring to the plate, then our value can be taken away. If it's based on how pretty we are, how talented we are, or how smart we are, what happens when we're not as pretty, talented, or smart? Does that mean our value has changed? If our value is based on those things, when they are taken away, so is our value!

However, the Bible tells us that God bases our value on what Jesus Christ did for us, and on who He says we are when we belong to Him. That changes everything. He told us that we are fearfully and wonderfully made (Psalm 139:14) and that we are literally knit together in our mother's womb (Psalm 139:13, NIV). The Bible tells us that God created man in His image (Genesis 1:27) and that man is the crowning glory of His creation (Psalm 8:5). That's who God says we are. And no person or circumstance can ever take that away."

I continued, "Now, did God want you or me to go through what we went through? No! God gave us what He wanted us to have, and that was perfection. When He was finished creating the world, everything wasn't just good; it was *very good*. That's what we have to look forward to when we see the new heaven and the new earth. The new heaven and the new earth will be a restoration of what life was like in the beginning: a place where we will experience no more tears, no more sorrow, and no more pain (Revelation 21:4). We are the ones who blew it. God gave us perfection, but man (Adam) sinned and so we are all born with a sin nature. We live in a fallen world, where all people sin. When we repent and trust in Jesus Christ, He forgives all our sins—past, present, and future—but He doesn't necessarily remove the consequences of sinful behavior. So we must deal with the consequences of sins we have committed and the sins that have been committed against us.

"But there's good news!" I told this young lady. "We can have hope because God loves us and has prepared a place for us to spend eternity with Him. Romans 5:3,4 says, 'And not only that, but we also glory in tribulations, knowing that tribulation produces perseverance; and perseverance, character; and character, hope.' When we have the proper perspective, God can and does use the things that have happened to us to bring glory to Him and to build our character, as hard as that is to believe sometimes."

I paused and told her gently, "I can now look you right in the eyes and tell you there is another way because of what I've experienced. God prepared me to be able to give hope to folks who may never listen to you. But God has prepared you, with what you've experienced, to bring hope to somebody who would never listen to me. The Bible makes it very clear that God will use the bad things in our lives to draw us closer to Him and to allow us to give hope to a world that doesn't know there is another way! It's up to you to choose which way you're going to go."

I wish I could say that this young lady fell on her face, repented and trusted Jesus as her Lord and Savior right then, but that didn't happen. However, I felt that the chip on her shoulder was gone after that. I led the discussion for about forty more minutes, and she paid attention and asked more questions without the edge in her voice. I still pray for all these young ladies, and I hope that the Lord will continue to comfort them, guide them, and lead them into a relationship with Himself.

Everywhere I go to speak, I find people who are excited and encouraged by my story. They realize that God can use anyone to do His work—even the messed-up son of a professional wrestler who ended up earning his livelihood as an air-traffic controller and then a public creation speaker.

My prayer is that these elements of my life story will inspire and encourage you to be confident in sharing what God has done for you. Most of all, I hope you will be challenged with the knowledge that the Word of God, from the beginning of Genesis to the end of Revelation, has all the answers we need today—not only for doctrine, but for our daily lives.

SEEING BEAUTY IN BROKEN PIECES

In 2010, Masami and I had the privilege of hosting a trip to Israel, which was an incredible experience. Our guide shared truths that really made the Word of God come alive for us. While we were in Israel, I was fascinated by the ancient mosaics. Whenever we visited the various architectural ruins, I would make a beeline for the mosaics because they were so intriguing to me. In one place the path that the people walked on was one massive mosaic that had been built over many times during the years. It was just amazing—the painstaking detail in these works of art contained so much beauty.

I'll never forget the time when I rounded a corner in Jerusalem and found myself face-to-face with a shop door surrounded by numerous finely detailed mosaics. From a distance of about three feet, I scanned it up and down, left and right, but had a hard time seeing what the pictures were supposed to be. I couldn't see what the design was because I was too close, so I began to back up to gain a better view. When I got about fifteen feet away from the mosaics, the pictures suddenly popped into focus and I could see the grand design.

Courtesy Todd Bolen/BiblePlaces.com

The Oil Press Art Gallery, Jewish Quarter Road, Jerusalem

While I stood there admiring these well-loved biblical stories depicted through broken pieces of stone, God gave me an important perspective on what I've been trying to convey to you. All the personal stories that I've shared have something in common. When I was going through difficult times in my life, I didn't enjoy them, and I didn't understand the point of them. I was too close to the situation, seeing my life from a narrow and nearsighted perspective. I tried to use my own limited, fallible human wisdom to understand why these tough circumstances were happening to me. Just as I couldn't begin to see the mosaic designs until I took a few steps back, I had to do the same thing with the struggles that I went through.

While I was in the throes of painful trials, I couldn't understand why I was suffering. But now, as I look back over my life from a different perspective, I can see why God has allowed me to encounter some of the challenges I've gone through. It's just as Romans 5:3,4 promises: through my tribulations, God was creating within me the desire and ability to give people *hope!*

When Masami and I were in Israel, I really wanted to buy a beautiful mosaic. We even visited a factory where craftsmen created them by hand. But I discovered that the mosaics I could afford were composed of larger bits of stones and fewer pieces, so they didn't have a lot of detail to them. The mosaics I was most interested in (but couldn't afford) were made up of thousands of tiny pieces of broken stone, intricately arranged to create a stunningly detailed picture. The more broken pieces, the more beautiful the picture.

Just as the most incredible and detailed mosaics are made up of many broken pieces, we all have broken pieces in our lives that God will use to create a beautiful mosaic for our good and His glory.

When you look back over your life, you may wonder why you had to go through some of the tough things you experienced. In fact, you may be wondering why you're going through a difficult time right now. But if you wait on the Lord and step back a little to see the bigger picture, you'll also begin to understand God's perspective on your situation.

God loves you so much that He sent His Son, Jesus, to die for you. God didn't want you to have to experience hardship, pain, loss, and death. He wanted mankind to have perfection, and that's what He originally gave us. But all of us chose to rebel against Him and destroy what He gave us. That's called sin. Thankfully, He still loves us and wants to have a relationship with us. So He offers us redemption by letting us choose to trust in Jesus as our Savior.

Mark Hall, a friend of mine, is a member of the Christian recording group Casting Crowns and helped to write the song "Voice of Truth." In this song he refers to the many voices that are constantly calling out to us and reminding us of the past failures in our lives. But, in the midst of all those negative, deceptive voices, there is one voice—that still, small voice—that speaks the truth, and that's the voice we need to listen to.

This song has resonated so strongly with me. At so many points in my life, I have failed miserably. Those negative, condemning, shaming voices still call to me, trying to drag me down and keep me from moving forward with faith in Jesus. I'm a new creation in Christ, but those voices try to tell me that I am still the old creation.

For me, it's a daily challenge to remember that I am not the person I used to be. That person is dead, spiritually speaking. God has made all things new. I have been redeemed by Jesus Christ, and now God is working in me to conform me into the image of Christ.

I'm praying that these stories based on the "stones" and "boulders" I've encountered in my life will encourage you to listen to the "voice of truth." And that truth is this: Jesus came to seek and save the lost (Luke 19:10). He died for our sins, was buried, and rose again from the dead (1 Corinthians 15:1–4), and He lives to make intercession for us (Hebrews 7:25). He loves us (John 15:9), He saved us (Acts 4:12), and He has justified us (Romans 3:24). He has cast our sins away, as far as the east is from the west (Psalm 103:12). He will never leave us or forsake us (Hebrews 13:5). He gives us the power to live for Him (2 Peter 1:3) and to be His witnesses (Acts 1:8). He has given us eternal life (John 5:24) and He is coming back again one day to receive us to Himself (John 14:3).

Just as the most incredible and detailed mosaics are made up of many broken pieces, we all have broken pieces in our lives that God will use to create a beautiful mosaic for our good and His glory (Romans 8:28; Hebrews 13:21). Ultimately, we will be able to gain the perfect and final perspective on the mosaic of our lives, in all of its intricate detail, from the vantage point of eternity. What a day that will be! We can have strength to press on today in anticipation of our glorious future.

In the meantime, I hope that you will be encouraged to use your own life stories and your own testimony, your mosaic, to share with others how God has taken the broken pieces of your life and made something beautiful and valuable. He continues to add to that mosaic each and every day. Watch for His hand in your life and always sanctify Him in your heart. I hope that you will always be a willing servant of God, for He will inspire and empower you to:

> ...be ready always to give an answer to every man that asketh you a reason of the hope that is in you with meekness and fear. (1 Peter 3:15, KJV)

Stay bold!

Epilogue

I am encouraged to tell you that God has brought about great healing in my life and in my family relationships through the writing of this book. About five years ago, I grew so frustrated with the relationship I had with my mother that I told Masami I was not going to reach out to my mom anymore. I struggled with being the one who always initiated contact and tried to maintain the relationship. I told Masami, "I'm tired of reaching out and not seeing anything come back. Relationships are a two-way street, and I just don't feel like she wants to be in touch with me."

For about a year, I didn't make any more calls to my mother. Then one Sunday, our pastor, Mike Jones, preached a sermon that really moved my wife. It was a powerful message about the importance of ministering to our immediate family. As a result, Masami encouraged me to reach out to my mother again. She was very persistent, so I agreed to make contact.

After I called my mom, she pulled together a fantastic family reunion that was a great blessing to everyone in attendance. That really began to improve our relationship.

After I finished this book, I sent my mother a copy of the manuscript to make sure my memory was accurate and to get her approval of her own story that I included in the book. Her response totally blessed me.

I share this with you because I want to tell you, "Don't do what I did! Don't give up on your loved ones." As Pastor Mike made very clear in his sermon that day, if we're not ministering to our families, we don't have a lot of right to minister to others.

I can honestly say that my mom's words were so affirming that it will not bother me if no one else ever reads this book! Her response means the world to me. I learned that God wants us to be reconciled in our relationships not only with Him, but with our families as well.

I'd like to share what my mother wrote:

This book is an incredible piece of work. I picked it up at around 5 last night and I could not put it down. Tuesday night is "NCIS" night. It's my all-time favorite TV show, and I never miss it. But last night I missed it! I read and read and read. I fell asleep at I don't know what time, when I was on page 175. I woke up at 4 this morning and knew I had to shower and get ready for the day before I started reading again, because I knew I would not put the book down until I had finished. I just finished!

Carl, this book is filled with so much hope and promise that there is no way that a person could not benefit from reading it. It puts so many things into perspective for me. I discovered through your words that the situations that I thought were punishments by God were actually gifts from Him instead.

I remember that day when you ran off to your Dad's. I was scared to death. I was so afraid he would just take you away and turn you into his little clone. By the time you got home I was so angry and afraid. I yelled at you, and I had no idea what a huge and painful decision you had made that day. I'm so ashamed. I am crying while I write this, just at the thought of how I treated you that day. I'm so truly sorry for that.

You inspire people, Carl, me included. I went to a friend's graduation party on Mother's Day. I don't remember how the subject of faith came up, but our beliefs became the topic of conversation. I didn't know I was going to enter the conversation, and I didn't say much, but I did say: "I am a Christian, and somewhat serious about it." That sounds rather weak right now, but after reading your book, I look at it as a start.

I look at what you have done and I can't tell you how very proud I am of you. Your family life is beautiful. I couldn't love your wife more if she were my own child. She is a rock and one of the most beautiful people I know.

This book needs to get into the hands of the masses. Hope is so desperately needed right now. Thank you for sharing this book with me. It's powerful, inspiring, and filled with hope.

I love you!

Mom

MY FINAL THOUGHTS

As I reflected on my mother's letter, it made me think about how many pieces of the mosaic of her life are also a part of my life's mosaic. And then I began to think how, as the body of Christ, believers are all a part of that great mosaic, the Church.

Mosaics are beautiful, and so is the Church. The mosaic of the Church is composed of many broken pieces—people from all walks of life who have been broken, and then restored by Christ and adorned with His righteousness. The mosaic of believers that compose the Church is also known as the bride of Christ. We are promised to Him, and given to Him by the Father, and we long for the day when the Bridegroom returns for us.

These thoughts of the Church as a great mosaic then took my mind's eye to the glorious vision described in the fourth chapter of the last book of the Bible, the book of Revelation.

Jesus Christ reveals to the apostle John the throne room of God, and John records:

> Immediately I was in the Spirit; and behold, a throne set
> in heaven, and One sat on the throne. And He who sat
> there was like a jasper and a sardius stone in appear-
> ance; and there was a rainbow around the throne, in
> appearance like an emerald. (Revelation 4:2,3)

Wow! A glorious mosaic like precious stones—jasper and
sardius, and a rainbow "like an emerald." As wonderful as that
sounds, John goes on to record an even more glorious sight
before his eyes:

> And I looked, and behold, in the midst of the throne
> and of the four living creatures, and in the midst of the
> elders, stood a Lamb as though it had been slain, having
> seven horns and seven eyes, which are the seven Spirits
> of God sent out into all the earth. (Revelation 5:6)

John sees Jesus! And He's described as the Lamb that was
sacrificed for our sins, "the Lamb of God who takes away the
sin of the world!" (John 1:29). John continues,

> Then I looked, and I heard the voice of many angels
> around the throne, the living creatures, and the elders;
> and the number of them was ten thousand times ten
> thousand, and thousands of thousands, saying with a
> loud voice:
>
> > "Worthy is the Lamb who was slain to receive
> > power and riches and wisdom, and strength and
> > honor and glory and blessing!"
>
> And every creature which is in heaven and on the earth
> and under the earth and such as are in the sea, and all
> that are in them, I heard saying:
>
> > "Blessing and honor and glory and power be to
> > Him who sits on the throne, and to the Lamb,
> > forever and ever!"

Then the four living creatures said, "Amen!" And the twenty-four elders fell down and worshiped Him who lives forever and ever. (Revelation 5:11–14)

What more can I say? That is the most glorious mosaic we will ever behold and our Lord has given us a small glimpse of it in His Word. The broken but redeemed—not just the Church, but the saints of all ages—will one day come together in heavenly worship of our Lord.

Focus your mind's eye on that heavenly mosaic and, until that day when we see Him face to face, continue to run the race—for your good and His glory.

And always hold fast to your Reason for Hope.*

*JESUS!

Now may the God of hope fill you with all joy and peace in believing, that you may abound in hope by the power of the Holy Spirit.
—Romans 15:13

Notes

1. "Mosaics," Montessori World Educational Institute <www.montessoriworld.org/Handwork/texture/texture3.html>.

2. Terry Tempest Williams, Finding Beauty in a Broken World (New York: Pantheon Books, 2008), 385.

3. After the Fall blog, November 25, 2010 <www.afterthefallministry.com/blog/blog.php?bid=82>.

4. How Craig dealt with the tragic turn in his life is documented in the video "After the Fall: A Climber's True Story of Facing Death and Relying on God."

5. David Kinnaman, "The Mosaic Generation: The Mystifying New World of Youth Culture," Enrichment Journal, Fall 2006 <www.enrichmentjournal.ag.org/200604/200604_028_MosaicGen.cfm>.

6. Ibid.

7. "2010 Census Data," U.S. Census Bureau <www.2010.census.gov/2010census/data>.

8. "Revere," Merriam-Webster Dictionary Online <www.merriam-webster.com/dictionary/revere>.

9. HELPS Word-studies, "Apologia" <www.concordances.org/greek/627.htm>.

10. Ibid.

11. Ryan Turner, "What is Apologetics? An Outline" <www.carm.org/apologetics-outline>.

12. Rosamund and Benjamin Zander, The Art of Possibility (New York: Penguin Books, 2002), 5–6.

13. Jon Walker, "Family Life Council Says It's Time to Bring Family Back to Life," Baptist Press, June 12, 2002 <www.bpnews.net/bpnews.asp?ID=13591>.

14. Voddie T. Baucham, Jr., Family Driven Faith: Doing What It Takes to Raise Sons and Daughters Who Walk with God (Wheaton, IL: Crossway Books, 2007), 22.

15. Rex Dalton, "In Search of Thingummyjigosaurus: There are errors in almost half the names given to dinosaurs," Nature, September 17, 2008 <www.nature.com/news/2008/080917/full/news.2008.1111.html>.

16. Lee Strobel, "How Apologetics Changed My Life," The Apologetics Study Bible (Nashville, TN: Holman, 2007), xxvi.

17. Natalie Angier, "Do Races Differ? Not Really, Genes Show," New York Times, August 22, 2000, 1(F).

18. Jasper Becker, The Chinese (Oxford: Oxford University Press, 2002), 233.

Notes

19. Stephen Jay Gould, *Ontogeny and Phylogeny* (Cambridge, MA: Belknap-Harvard University Press, 1977), 127–128.

20. Chuck Colson, "Bosnia and Biopolitics: Did Violence Evolve?" *BreakPoint*, April 6, 1993 <www.breakpoint.org/commentaries/3561-bosnia-and-biopolitics>.

21. "Prejudice Is Hard-Wired into the Human Brain, Says ASU Study," *ScienceDaily*, May 25, 2005 <www.sciencedaily.com/releases/2005/05/050525105357.htm>.

22. Rick Groleau, "Tracing Ancestry with MtDNA," Nova/PBS <www.pbs.org/wgbh/nova/neanderthals/mtdna.html>.

23. Hillary Mayell, "Geneticist Searches for DNA of 'Adam,' the First Human," *National Geographic News*, June 24, 2005 <http://news.nationalgeographic.com/news/2005/06/0624_050624_spencerwells.html>.

24. Carl Wieland, "Darwin's Bodysnatchers: New Horrors," *Creation*, March 1992, 16–18 <www.creation.com/darwins-bodysnatchers-new-horrors>.

25. Nicholas Glass, "Fight for ancestoral remains," Channel 4 News Special Report, London, October 8, 2003.

26. Edwin Black, *War Against the Weak* (New York: Four Walls, Eight Windows, 2003), xvi.

27. Ibid.

28. Shari Rudavsky, "Looking at the History of Eugenics in Indiana," *The Indianapolis Star*, April 13, 2007.

29. Jerry Bergman, "The Church Preaches Eugenics: A History of Church Support for Darwinism and Eugenics," *Journal of Creation* 20(3), 2006, 57.

30. Beth J. Lueders, "Coming Alongside a Suicidal Teen," TroubledWith (Focus on the Family), 2004.

31. "Teenage Suicide," National Alliance on Mental Illness <www.nami.org/Content/ContentGroups/Helpline1/Teenage_Suicide.htm>.

32. John Bunyan, Preface to *Grace Abounding to the Chief of Sinners* <www.gutenberg.org/dirs/etext96/gacos10h.htm>.

Resources

For additional information to help you share the reasons for your hope, see the following resources:

- **Becoming Bold: Know It! Live It! Share It! conference on DVD**: Messages that will challenge, equip, and encourage you to grow in your faith and be bold in your witness for Christ.

- **Q&A Live at Cedar Creek**: An information-rich DVD with answers to some of today's most difficult questions.

- **deBunked videos**: Fast-paced, hard-hitting, fun, and entertaining, these 3-minute videos creatively debunk lies by providing truths about Christianity and the Bible.

- **Real-Life Evangelism DVD Series**: Wherever God has placed you, learn to effectively evangelize.

Carl Kerby has available numerous books, DVDs, tracts, and homeschool materials. For a complete list of resources, to sign up for our free enewsletter, or to support the ministry, please visit www.rforh.com.

To request a speaking engagement, contact 800-552-HOPE (4673) or visit www.rforh.com/book-a-speaker.

Contact Carl at:

Reasons for Hope
P.O. Box 415
Hebron, KY 41048
800-552-HOPE (4673)
www.rforh.com
info@rforh.com